P9-DWU-820

Spreads, Toppers, & Dips

SPREADS,

TOPPERS,

& DIPS

Diane Rozas

THIS BOOK IS THE PROPERTY OF
THE NATIONAL CITY PUBLIC LIBRARY

MACMILLAN • USA

This book is dedicated to Kevin, for all his support. Special thanks
to Karen Schafer for coordinating and Amy Gordon for her editorial vision.

MACMILLAN
A Simon & Schuster Macmillan Company
1633 Broadway
New York, NY 10019-6785

Copyright © 1997 by Diane Rozas

All rights reserved. No part of this book may be reproduced or transmitted in
any form by any means, electronic or mechanical, including photocopying,
recording, or by any information storage and retrieval system, without
permission in writing from the Publisher.

MACMILLAN is a registered trademark of Macmillan, Inc.

Library of Congress Cataloging-in-Publication Data

Rozas, Diane.
        Spreads, toppers, & dips / by Diane Rozas.
            p. cm.
        Includes index.
        ISBN 0-02-861003-2 (alk. paper)
        1. Appetizers.   2. Dips (Appetizers)   I. Title.
TX740.R65   1997   96-39679
641.8'12—dc21   CIP

Printed in the United States of America

10 9 8 7 6 5 4 3 2 1

BOOK DESIGN BY HEATHER KERN

ILLUSTRATIONS BY SHIRLEY A. KERN

Contents

Introduction

It seems that spreads, toppers, and dips are more popular than ever these days—as appetizers in restaurants; as quick, delicious, small meals at home; or as snacks on the run. At your favorite market or take-out deli you've probably noticed some of these tasty items sold by the pound, like hummus dip, fresh salsa, and rich guacamole.

What exactly are these tasty and convenient foods? Outright delicious edibles to spread on bread, pile on crackers, top baked potatoes, and scoop up with a chip or wedges of raw vegetable.

Unless you've been living a reclusive lifestyle, you've possibly encountered spreads and toppers and dips as the newest wave in party fare. Typical hors d'oeuvres or appetizer assortments are frequently a selection of spreads, toppers, and dips of contrasting tastes and textures. Some of the most popular include herb-infused wine and cheese spread, fish mousse, black olive tapenade, and silky roasted garlic purée. These sumptuous substances are presented in crocks, bowls, and terrines and surrounded by an assortment of accompaniments, such as crispy toast pieces, crackers, crudités, and a variety of chips. Obviously, there is a lot of flexibility when it comes to fitting perfectly with any occasion, taste, or budget. So it's no wonder this delightful way of tasting and nibbling one's way across a buffet table is dominating the entertaining scene these days. Besides, it's fun to eat this way.

Spreads, Toppers, & Dips offers all the standards, plus many new versatile yet sophisticated recipes that are easy to make, impressive to serve, and surprisingly economical. These 161 recipes and 49 variations fit into everyday meals as well as menus for entertaining. And not only do they offer opportunities to experience a "fusion" of ethnic flavors, but they also are every bit as delicious as similar dishes sold at gourmet take-out shops or served at a catered soirée. Perhaps better. And you'll get all the credit.

These days, with the renaissance of hearty country-style and hearth-baked breads, there are situations when plain butter or even a saucer of olive oil just doesn't do the trick. Many of the spreads and toppers in this book are a much better match with a slice of bread made with dark olives, sweet raisins, or seeds and nuts, or perfumed with fresh rosemary, speckled with sun-dried tomatoes, or created from hundred-year-old sourdough starter. And with myriad stores, from corner bakeries to health food emporiums to supermarkets, now stocking an array of ethnic flatbreads, including tortillas and pitas, topping them properly makes a delicious and impressive presentation. This book provides the right recipes for ethnic-flavored spreads, toppers, and dips. So whether you're a traditionalist or would rather make your own creative match-ups, herein you'll find plenty of inspiration.

Recently in a local restaurant, I found myself faced with an assortment of wildly colored and interestingly textured substances placed beside the bread basket—exactly where the butter used to go. Although I knew I would soon be slathering these spreadables on one (or several) of the delicious pieces of breads waiting in the basket, I called the waiter to quench my curiosity. "What's all this?" I naively asked before I plunged in my knife. His description exceeded my wildest expectations. As he named each item on the sampler tray (some of the mixtures were no doubt low in fat), he also informed me I could use them to spread on, top off, or dredge through the piece of walnut and raisin-specked dark bread that I held in my hand. "Butternut squash and tahini, sweet potato purée, white bean pâté with herbs," he spouted out in rapid succession. Then, continuing at the same pace, he added, "We also have sprouted beans, seeds, and nut spread, Southwestern guacamole, and sautéed spinach and goat cheese. Wanna try some?" I politely said, "Oh, maybe later." But what I really meant was "Yes, let me try them all, right now! What tastes! What textures! What imagination! How could I have ever been satisfied with plain old boring butter on my bread? Never again! From now on, I'm for spreads. And toppers and dips, too."

The next morning I set to work reinterpreting several of those tasty creations while the flavors were still lingering in my memory. Many are here among this collection of 161 new and well-loved recipes. End of story? Not quite.

So, if you still think a "dip" is something made with sour cream and dehydrated vegetable flecks, a "spread" is swirled fluorescent-orange cheese whip, and a "topper" means shake-on bacon bits, then it's time for you to taste your way through this book.

Taste this with your imagination: Smoked Salmon Fromage scooped up with an endive spear.

Now try this: Fruit and Spice Mascarpone Spread on a chubby breakfast bun.

Here, think about a bite of these: Lemony Low-Fat Garbanzo or Lentil Hummus scooped up with Spice Pita Chips or a salted twisty pretzel.

Now dream of tasting this: Polenta Crisps with silky smooth Gorgonzola and Grappa Spread, or Honey-Baked Ham and Cheddar Spread on an herb and olive oil–roasted potato wedge.

Just one last delicious (and torturous) treat to try with the powers of your mind: colorful and crisp Homemade Vegetable Chips (I mean beet, carrot, parsnip, sweet potato) with a dollop of Eggplant Caviar or dredged through creamy Golden Caviar Spread.

If your appetite has suddenly come alive, the need to throw a party for all your best food-loving friends has struck, or you're dreaming of all the new enticing edible additions to your low-fat, healthy, or vegetarian lifestyle, then it's time to think in terms of spreads, toppers, and dips. For all occasions, from everyday eating to elegant entertaining . . . or right now!

Essential Ingredients

One of the essentials for making spreads, toppers, and dips anytime is the availability of ingredients. My personal approach is to gather all the essentials I might need to put together an assortment of hors d'oeuvres, and then I make sure to keep the stock replenished. So when it's snack time or cocktail time and a few people have gathered around, I won't be zipping out to the store in my car for ingredients. Instead, I'll be putting out a wonderful-tasting spread or topper or dip with golden, crusty bread or crisp crackers.

To start, choose the spreads, toppers, and dips you love the most, and make a shopping list of all the ingredients. Pin it to the inside of the cupboard. Check the list and replenish the ingredients whenever you go to the store. The art of shopping for a party menu is really no different—just increase the amounts accordingly.

Consider having some or all of these ingredients on hand for spreads, toppers, and dips:

Pantry

honey

sugar

canned fish (tuna, salmon, crab, anchovies, mackerel)

tomatoes (canned), whole or crushed

sun-dried tomatoes

refried beans (canned)

chickpeas (garbanzo beans), dried and canned

chilies (canned), green and chipotle

olives: green and black in water; oil-cured

small capers

olive oil (extra virgin), strong and light flavors

oils: safflower, canola, vegetable, sesame oil (light and dark), walnut and hazelnut

vinegars: balsamic, red wine, white wine, or champagne

mayonnaise: reduced-fat and regular

tahini

nuts: blanched almonds, hazelnuts, walnuts, pistachios, peanuts

seeds: sunflower seeds, sesame seeds

Asian ingredients: fish sauce, chili sauce with garlic, dried mushrooms, dried Thai shrimp

Refrigerator and Freezer

sour cream (low-fat and
  nonfat if desired)
cream cheese (regular and
  low-fat; nonfat if desired)
ricotta (part-skim), yogurt
  (low-fat)
fresh and aged chèvre, or goat
  cheese (see sidebar, page 23)
Parmesan or romano cheese
  (chunk or freshly grated)
milk (low-fat and regular),
  buttermilk

mushrooms: wild and
  cultivated
Roasted Garlic Purée
  (see page 3 for recipe)
several pestos in tightly
  sealed containers (see pages
  113–116 for recipes)
frozen fresh sliced French
  or Italian bread (baguettes),
  stored in plastic bags
frozen artichoke hearts

Fresh Herbs

basil
chervil
cilantro
dill

mint
oregano
parsley (flat-leaf)

Spices, Dried Herbs and Condiments

coriander
cumin
red pepper flakes
chili powder
cayenne
paprika
curry powder or paste
Indian mixed spices
  (garam masala)
garlic powder
dried basil
dried dill
dried oregano
dried tarragon
dried thyme

herbes de Provence (thyme,
  summer savory, rosemary,
  and lavender)
fines herbes (oregano, sage,
  rosemary, marjoram, and
  basil)
salt, pepper, herb, and spice
  blends (make your own or
  choose a few commercial
  mixes: Caribbean, Creole,
  garlic pepper, etc.)
black and white peppercorns
  in separate peppermills
table salt and coarse salt
soy sauce (low-salt, light,
  and dark)

Vegetable Bin

beets
broccoli florets
cauliflower florets
celery
garlic (several whole heads)
onions: white, red, and yellow;
  sweet onions (Maui,
    Walla Walla, or Vidalia)

potatoes: Idaho, yellow fin
  or yukon, and purple;
  sweet potatoes
shallots
tomatillos
acorn or butternut squash
zucchini

Liquor Cabinet (for cooking)

beer
wine (dry white and red)
vermouth (dry)
champagne (brut)
sherry (dry and medium)
brandy or cognac, grappa

liqueurs: kirsch,
  Grand Marnier, ouzo,
  Pernod
Scotch
vodka

Techniques and Equipment

Techniques

Blanch.   Boil water in a large pot, then immerse vegetables completely in the water for several seconds or as much as 1 minute, depending on the vegetable. This process takes the bitterness out of vegetables and gives them a tender, crunchy texture. After blanching, run the vegetables under cold tap water or transfer to a bowl with ice water to stop the cooking process.

Bread crumbs (fresh).   Cut the crusts from ordinary white bread. Tear into small pieces and place in the bowl of a food processor fitted with the metal blade. Process until fluffy crumbs fill the bottom of the bowl. Use immediately or make into dried bread crumbs.

Bread crumbs (dried).   Spread fresh bread crumbs (see above) on a baking sheet in a single layer. Place in a 250°F oven for 10 to 12 minutes or until dried. Transfer to the bowl of a food processor fitted with the metal blade. Process into crumbs or crush slightly between wax paper with a rolling pin.

Chopping.   Many ingredients require chopping. A good sharp knife that is fairly heavy in weight and well balanced is one of the few pieces of quality equipment you will need. Several cutting boards in a variety of sizes are very helpful as well.

Grinding spices.   If you plan to grind your own spices for each use, toast whole spices in a pan over high heat for a few seconds, and then place in a coffee grinder (reserved for grinding spices) and grind to a fine powder.

Peeling and seeding tomatoes.   Boil water in a large saucepan and dip tomatoes in, one at a time, for about 20 to 30 seconds or until the skin begins to pucker. Run under cold water and peel off the skin easily. Or place the tomatoes in a colander and pour boiling water over them. After about 1 minute, rinse with cold water to stop the cooking process, then remove the skins easily. To seed, cut the tomatoes in half, squeeze very gently, and the seeds will come right out. Use a spoon to scrape out any that remain.

Reducing liquids.　This is the simple process of boiling down a liquid, such as stock, to concentrate the flavor. In a saucepan over high heat, boil the liquid, watching carefully, until it is reduced to the desired amount.

Roasting tomatoes, onions, garlic, and shallots.　In a 375°F oven, heat 1 to 2 tablespoons of olive oil in a large roasting pan. Add the vegetables to the pan and shake to coat lightly with oil. Roast 45 minutes to 1 hour. When done, garlic, onions, and shallots should be soft throughout; tomatoes should be blackened on the outside. Remove from the oven. When cool enough to handle, peel and discard all skins.

Seeding and roasting bell peppers.　Cut the peppers in half and remove the seeds and veins if necessary. Broil cut-side down (or place on a grill or gas flame cut side up) until blackened. Place in a paper or plastic bag and let sit for 10 to 15 minutes. Remove from the bag and peel the skin off the peppers.

Seeding, deveining, and roasting chilies.　Wear rubber gloves when handling fresh chilies. Any contact with the oils from chilies can cause burning. Stem and cut the chile open lengthwise and spread it out flat. Using the tip of a knife, scrape away the white inner veins as well as the seeds and discard. Place the chile in a glass dish and wash the utensils and surfaces that came in contact with the chile and its fiery oils. Then you may remove your gloves. To roast a chile, blacken the skin until it blisters under the broiler, over a grill, or even over the flame on a gas stovetop. Place the chile in a paper bag and quickly roll down the top to seal and keep in the steam. When the chile cools, while wearing rubber gloves, remove it and peel off the charred skin immediately. Discard the skin.

Storing fresh bread in the freezer.　Fresh loaves of bread can be cut into slices and immediately frozen in zipper-lock bags for later use.

Toasting nuts.　Place the nuts on a baking sheet in a 400°F oven until browned, about 3 to 5 minutes. Watch carefully, as nuts cook quickly. To remove the skins from hazelnuts, after toasting, wrap them in a dish towel. Rub back and forth over the towel vigorously to loosen the skins.

Toasting seeds.　Place the seeds in a large, heavy skillet on the stovetop over high heat. Stir constantly, as they burn quickly and easily. When the seeds pop, remove them from the pan right away and spread on a plate to cool.

Equipment

Food processor.   This is a must. It provides the quickest, easiest method of preparing many of the recipes in this book. It is used for chopping, mincing, combining, and smoothing mixtures into pastes, spreads, purées, and the like. The mini food processor is a great addition to your collection of kitchen appliances and is often more efficient for combining small amounts, a frequent step in many recipes. A blender just can't do the work of a food processor, but in some cases it will suffice.

Mandoline.   This tabletop vegetable slicer can be used to create thin slices of vegetables for chips. (Or use a very sharp, heavy-bladed knife or the blade side of a steel grater.)

Nonstick pans.   Although they are optional, no kitchen should really be without a nonstick large skillet and medium sauté pan. You can spray a nonstick pan with vegetable oil cooking spray to cut the amount of oil used in some recipes and in general to cook lighter.

Ready for Every Occasion

The following useful categories are designed to make recipe select-ing easy. Use this section as a first step to finding recipes that con-tain all of the ingredients and qualities you require for a particular type of occasion or situation. As your favorite spreads, toppers, and dips emerge, start a category list of your own.

EVERYDAY FAVORITES

PARTY FARE

Party Classics

Casual Entertaining

Al Fresco Entertaining

Special Occasions

▫ QUICK AND EASY ▫

BETTER THAN BUTTER

LOW-FAT AND NONFAT

▫ HOT AND SPICY ▫

▫ THE BASICS ▫

The Accompaniments: What to Dunk With, Slather Onto, and Pile on Top of

When you've got the time to make your own chips, crackers, croûtes, and the like, there are plenty of delicious—and easy—homemade accompaniment recipes in the back of this book. When you're in a hurry or expecting last-minute guests, however, choose the following tasty premade or packaged accompaniments, which you can keep on hand in your pantry.

Bagel chips.   Already sliced, flavored, and toasted, bagel chips are available from your supermarket or perhaps your local bagel shop. Sure match-ups for this low-fat cracker substitute are Basic Pesto Dip (page 116), Garlic and Herb Cheese Spread (page 22), and Classic Tuna Spread (page 43).

Biscotti.   When a light sweet is required, choose biscotti. They're easy to make but time-consuming. So buy them already made at a bakery, gourmet store, or supermarket. A natural dunking tool; just plunge one into Fruit Purée (page 50) or Chocolate Espresso Spread (page 52).

Focaccia, baguette, or rustic or country-style breads and rolls.   You can tell if a bread is handmade and probably hearth-oven baked by the uneven shape of a slice. Serve the bread untoasted and topped with Provençal Eggplant Spread (page 133). For bruschetta and crostini recipes, see the Homemade Accompaniments chapter.

Crumpets, English muffins, scones, and buttermilk biscuits. Toasted wedges of bakery-fresh breads and muffins make perfect accompaniments to homemade Fruit Purée (page 50). Freshly baked biscuits and tiny corn muffins are enhanced by the flavors of pesto, sun-dried tomatoes, and goat cheese, which are included in such recipes as Fresh Herb Pestos (pages 113–115), Sun-Dried Tomato and Olive Tapenade (page 62), and Goat Cheese and Chutney Spread (page 24).

Fresh fruit wedges.   Apple and pear slices are especially good with a dollop of Chicken Liver and Hazelnut Pâté (page 45).

Dried fruit slices.   Readily available at health food stores, dried fruit slices are usually air-dried. Serve them whenever fruit flavors match up—for example, with a variety of wine and cheese spreads, including St. André and Armagnac (page 17).

Naan (Indian flatbread).   The authentic naan breads are best bought at an Indian food store or restaurant, as they are cooked in a unique fashion—a whole loaf is stuck to the inside of the tandoori oven to bake. Heat naan before serving if desired. It's great with Curried Squash Spread (page 39).

Japanese shrimp chips, little rice cakes, wasabi chips.   Wonders await in Japanese markets. Puffs and crisps of a variety of flavors, shapes, and colors add an element of playfulness to the hors d'oeuvre presentation. Serve alongside Pacific Rim Guacamole (page 138) or Fresh Tuna and Wasabi (page 97).

Matzoh and lavash.   Available in most supermarkets, these crisp crackers now range in flavors and can accompany plain or fancy spreads or toppers such as Layered Ricotta Terrine (page 72).

Pretzels.   Dredge a twisty one through Hummus (page 118).

Pita.   Buy white or wheat pita bread pockets and slice into triangular shapes. Serve with Fresh Herb and Avocado Fromage Topper (page 73). To make Herb or Spice Pita Chips, see page 162.

Tempura vegetables.   Just buy a box of tempura mix from the supermarket or from an Asian food market, turn the box over, and follow the directions. Then serve the lightly fried vegetables with Spicy Bell Pepper Purée (page 140) or Mint and Parsley Chutney (page 58).

Vegetable chips.   Called Terra Chips, these relatively new additions to the chips shelf are delightful looking and tasting, but expensive. In the bag are a variety of interesting flavors. (But with a little time and effort, you can easily make your own carrot, beet, parsnip, and sweet potato chips. See page 168 for the recipe.) Homemade or from the bag, these colorful and delicious chips make unique accompaniments for such toppers and dips as Cucumber and Yogurt Topper (Tzatziki) (page 77), Taramasalata (page 143), or any Cheese, Cream, and Yogurt Dip (pages 125–131).

Crackers. A mind-boggling array of crackers is available in endless flavors—cracked wheat, whole wheat, oat, rye, sesame, graham. Keep a few different kinds on hand to match up with cheese and meat spreads and toppers.

Spreads

For recipes using this Spread, see pages 6, 22, 28, 65, 71, 128, and 139.

Roasted Garlic Purée

Makes about 1 cup

4 large heads of garlic
$^1/_4$ cup defatted chicken broth (homemade or canned)
2 tablespoons extra virgin olive oil
$1^1/_4$ teaspoons dried herbes de Provence or equal parts of dried thyme,
marjoram, sage or summer savory, rosemary, and lavender
Pinch of salt
Pinch of freshly ground white pepper

1. Preheat the oven to 400°F.

2. With a sharp knife, cut off and discard the tops of the garlic heads, exposing a small amount of all the cloves. Peel off and discard any loose papery outer skin, leaving most in place.

3. Set the garlic heads, root side down, in a small ovenproof saucepan with a metal handle and tight-fitting lid, or in a baking dish lined with a piece of aluminum foil large enough to form a sealed package, and hold the heads of garlic so they are barely touching.

4. Drizzle the broth and olive oil evenly over the garlic, then sprinkle $^1/_4$ teaspoon of the dried herbs over each head.

5. Cover the saucepan and place in the oven, or if using a baking dish, wrap the foil to form a tightly sealed package. Bake until the inner cloves are very soft, about 1 hour. Remove the lid or foil cover and let cool to room temperature.

6. Squeeze the soft garlic pulp out of the heads into a small bowl. Discard the skins. Mash with a fork until creamy and smooth. Add salt and pepper and the remaining $^1/_4$ teaspoon dried herbs and stir to combine. Transfer to a crock or serving bowl. Serve immediately or transfer to a jar with a tight-fitting lid and refrigerate until ready to serve.

Spread this nutty, almost sweet-flavored puree on slices of country-style bread instead of butter. Use this to finish off a spread such as homemade mayonnaise, or add to an herb vinaigrette or a pasta sauce.

Caramelized Onion and Herb Spread

Makes about 1 cup

This low-fat sandwich spread is also an interesting alternative to butter.

Try 2 or more tablespoons on a white or sweet baked potato.

6 to 8 cloves garlic, peeled
3 tablespoons extra virgin olive oil
1 large yellow onion, sliced into $1/3$-inch rounds
2 scallions, white and some green parts, finely chopped
2 tablespoons finely chopped flat-leaf parsley
1 teaspoon crushed dried rosemary, herbes de Provence,
   or prepared seasoning mix of choice
Salt
Freshly ground black pepper

1. Place the garlic cloves in a small saucepan with a tight-fitting lid. Drizzle with 1 tablespoon of the olive oil and shake the pan to distribute the oil. Cover the pan and cook over very low heat until the cloves are soft, 10 to 12 minutes.

2. Meanwhile, in a heavy skillet, heat the remaining olive oil over medium-high heat. Cook the onions in a flat, even layer until browned and caramelized, about 15 minutes. Do not stir or move the onions, but press down on top of the layer with a spatula from time to time. Turn the entire layer over like a pancake to brown and caramelize the other side. Cook for about 10 minutes more. Remove from the heat.

3. Remove the garlic from the saucepan to paper towels to absorb any excess oil. Place the garlic cloves in the bowl of a food processor fitted with the metal blade. Process to a smooth paste.

4. Add the onion and process to a purée. Add the scallions, parsley, and herbs or seasoning mix and process briefly to blend. Season to taste with salt and pepper.

5. Transfer to a serving bowl and serve immediately. Or cover with plastic wrap, refrigerate, and serve chilled.

Herb and Spice Butters

Serve these flavored butters with warm bread, on toast, atop baked potatoes—anytime a savory alternative to plain butter is desired. For an interesting approach, offer several of these butters at once with an assortment of bread and dinner rolls before dinner. Choose ones that have contrasting colors, such as Roasted Red Bell Pepper Butter alongside Fresh Herb Butter, to add a festive look to the bread basket.

Roasted Shallot and Caper Butter

Makes about 1 cup

8 shallots, roasted (see page xiv) and peeled
1 cup (2 sticks) chilled unsalted butter, cut into pieces
1 teaspoon small capers, well rinsed, drained, and patted dry
Pinch of salt
Pinch of freshly ground black pepper

1. In the bowl of a food processor fitted with the metal blade, process all ingredients to a smooth paste.

2. Press into a crock or ramekin, cover with plastic wrap, refrigerate, and serve chilled.

Roasted Red Bell Pepper Butter

Makes about 1 cup

$^1/_2$ cup diced roasted, peeled, and seeded red bell pepper (see page xiv)
1 cup (2 sticks) chilled unsalted butter, cut into pieces
1 teaspoon freshly cracked black peppercorns
Pinch of salt

1. In the bowl of a food processor fitted with the metal blade, process all ingredients to a smooth paste.

2. Press into a crock or ramekin, cover with plastic wrap, refrigerate, and serve chilled.

Roasted Garlic and Green Peppercorn Butter

Makes about 1 cup

3 to 4 tablespoons Roasted Garlic Purée (page 3)
1 cup (2 sticks) chilled unsalted butter, cut into pieces
1 tablespoon green peppercorns (see Note), well rinsed, drained,
   and patted dry
Pinch of salt
Pinch of freshly ground black pepper

1. In the bowl of a food processor fitted with the metal blade, process all ingredients to a smooth paste.

2. Press into a crock or ramekin, cover with plastic wrap, refrigerate, and serve chilled.

Note: Unlike black or white peppercorns, green peppercorns are soft and are usually preserved in vinegar.

Fresh Herb Butter

Makes about 1 cup

1 cup (2 sticks) chilled unsalted butter, cut into pieces
$1/2$ cup chopped mixed fresh herbs, such as basil, chervil, flat-leaf parsley,
   oregano, tarragon, and chives
$1/2$ teaspoon grated lemon zest or fresh ginger
Pinch of salt
Pinch of freshly ground black pepper

1. In the bowl of a food processor fitted with the metal blade, process all ingredients to a smooth paste.

2. Press into a crock or ramekin, cover with plastic wrap, refrigerate, and serve chilled.

Spice Butter

Makes about 1 cup

1 cup (2 sticks) chilled unsalted butter, cut into pieces
1 tablespoon spice(s) of choice, such as mild or hot curry powder, mild paprika,
   dry mustard (use 1 teaspoon), a combination of cinnamon, nutmeg, ginger,
   and cloves, or a prepared spice mix such as Cajun or Caribbean, or to taste
1 teaspoon honey, or to taste (optional)
Pinch of salt
Pinch of freshly ground black pepper

1. In the bowl of a food processor fitted with the metal blade, process the butter, spices, honey, if using, salt, and pepper to a smooth paste.

2. Press into a crock or ramekin, cover with plastic wrap, refrigerate, and serve chilled.

Spicy Salsa Butter

Makes about 1 cup

1 cup (2 sticks) chilled unsalted butter, cut into pieces
1/2 cup well-drained Spicy Fresh Tomato Salsa (page 80)
Pinch of cayenne pepper (optional)
Pinch of salt

1. In the bowl of a food processor fitted with the metal blade, process the butter, salsa, cayenne pepper, if using, and salt to a smooth paste.

2. Press into a crock or individual ramekins, cover with plastic wrap, refrigerate, and serve chilled.

Sprouted Spread

Makes about $1^1/_2$ cups

Sprouted beans, peas, and nuts are usually available at a local farmers' market or at health food stores. Often they are found in grocery stores in the salad section, along with the long-forgotten bean sprouts.

2 ounces firm tofu, drained
2 tablespoons tahini
$^1/_4$ cup sprouted sunflower seeds
1 clove garlic, finely chopped
$^1/_2$ medium red onion, or 3 scallions, white part only, chopped
2 to 3 teaspoons Jensen's Vegetable Seasoning (see Note)
$^1/_4$ teaspoon salt
$^1/_8$ teaspoon cayenne pepper
1 to 2 tablespoons vegetable broth, or more as needed
$^1/_3$ cup sprouted red lentils
$^1/_3$ cup sprouted brown lentils
$^1/_3$ cup sprouted adzuki beans or other sprouted seeds, beans, or nuts, including peas, mung beans, black-eyed peas, almonds, and peanuts
3 tablespoons finely chopped flat-leaf parsley

1. In the bowl of a food processor fitted with the metal blade, combine the tofu, tahini, sunflower seeds, garlic, onion or scallions, vegetable seasoning, salt, and cayenne. Pulse several times to mix well, then continue processing, adding the vegetable broth 1 tablespoon at a time to thin the mixture. Process to a smooth spread.

2. Transfer to a medium mixing bowl. Stir in the sprouted lentils and other sprouted beans, seeds, and nuts. Stir in 2 tablespoons of the parsley. Adjust seasoning to taste with more salt.

3. Transfer to a serving bowl and sprinkle with the remaining parsley. Serve at room temperature or cover with plastic wrap, refrigerate, and serve chilled.

Note: Jensen's Vegetable Seasoning and similar vegetable protein-based seasoning products are available at health food stores.

Spicy Black Bean Spread

Makes about 1¹/₄ cups

One 16-ounce can black beans, rinsed, drained, and patted dry
¹/₂ cup freshly made Tomato Poblano Salsa (page 84) or fresh salsa from the deli section, well drained
2 tablespoons coarsely chopped cilantro
¹/₄ teaspoon ground cumin
¹/₄ teaspoon salt
¹/₄ teaspoon freshly ground black pepper
2 tablespoons finely diced green bell pepper
2 tablespoons finely diced yellow bell pepper
2 tablespoons finely diced red bell pepper

1. In the bowl of a food processor fitted with the metal blade, process the beans to a smooth consistency.

2. Add the salsa, cilantro, cumin, salt, and pepper and process just to mix, leaving some small chunks of tomato, if desired.

3. Stir in 1 tablespoon each of the green, yellow, and red bell peppers.

4. Transfer to a serving bowl. Sprinkle with the remaining bell peppers. Serve at room temperature.

Variation

Creamy Black Bean Spread

Increase the cumin to ¹/₂ teaspoon. Add ¹/₄ cup sour cream at the end of step 2. Adjust the seasoning to taste with salt and pepper.

Serve this spicy spread with warmed flour tortillas, crackers, or a variety of chips, especially tortilla chips. For a quick yet hearty snack, spread on tortilla chips, top with jack cheese, and broil for 30 seconds until the cheese melts. Sprinkle with the remaining bell peppers.

Italian White Bean Pâté

Makes about 1¹/₄ cups

This makes a flavorful butter substitute, especially if you're serving a basket of interesting breads before a meal. Fill a ramekin with this smooth thyme- and garlic-scented spread and place in the basket.

1 cup dried cannellini beans, soaked overnight in water, or 3 cups (24 ounces) canned cannellini or Great Northern beans, rinsed and drained
4 cups lightly salted chicken broth (if using dried beans)
1 teaspoon chicken broth or water, or more as needed
2 tablespoons extra virgin olive oil
2 teaspoons finely chopped fresh thyme, or ¹/₂ teaspoon dried
1 clove garlic, finely chopped
1 tablespoon finely chopped flat-leaf parsley
1 scallion, white and light green parts, chopped
¹/₂ teaspoon salt
¹/₄ teaspoon freshly ground black pepper, plus a few turns of the peppermill for garnish

1. If using dried beans, drain water after soaking. Place in a medium, heavy saucepan, add the chicken broth, and simmer over low heat until tender; check after 30 minutes for doneness. Drain and cool. If using canned beans, skip this step and continue with step 2.

2. In the bowl of a food processor fitted with the metal blade, combine the beans, the teaspoon of broth or water, olive oil, thyme, and garlic and process to a smooth consistency, adding more liquid until the desired consistency forms. (If made with canned beans the pâté will have a smoother, silkier consistency than pâté made with freshly cooked beans.)

3. Add all but 1 teaspoon of the parsley, the scallion, and salt and pepper. Pulse to mix. Transfer to a serving bowl. Top with a few turns of the peppermill and the remaining parsley. Serve at room temperature.

Fresh Fava Bean and Rosemary Spread

Makes about 1 ¹/₂ cups

2 cups shelled fresh fava beans (about 2 pounds unshelled), blanched (see Note)
1 clove garlic, finely chopped
1 teaspoon finely chopped fresh rosemary, or ¹/₂ teaspoon dried, crushed
¹/₂ cup extra virgin olive oil
2 tablespoons fresh lemon juice
Salt
Freshly ground black pepper

1. In the bowl of a food processor fitted with the metal blade, combine the beans, garlic, and rosemary. Process to a coarse purée.

2. Add half of the olive oil, the lemon juice, and salt and pepper to taste. Process, adding more oil as needed, to make a smooth spread.

3. Transfer to a serving bowl. Serve at room temperature.

Note: To prepare the fava beans, split the whole bean pod along the inside curve. Pick out the individual beans and discard the pods. Blanch the beans in lightly salted boiling water for 1 minute. Let cool, then peel off the tough outer skins.

Variations

For a creamier spread, reduce the oil to ¹/₄ cup, add ¹/₄ cup freshly grated Parmesan cheese and 2 tablespoons of sour cream at the end, and pulse to mix well. Serve immediately.

Sautéed Fava Bean Purée

Sauté shelled, blanched, and skinned fava beans and garlic with a pinch of dried herbs of choice in a little olive oil until tender, about 10 minutes. Add a little water during cooking if needed. Process to a spreading consistency and season to taste with salt and freshly ground pepper.

Tiny, rustic croûtes, or slices of grilled peasant bread can be smothered with this pale green, delicate, buttery-smooth bean spread. Fava beans are most typically found at farm stands in the summer months.

Oven-Dried Tomato and Pinto Bean Spread

Makes about 1 1/2 cups

Oven-dried tomatoes are not the hard, shriveled tomatoes known as sun-dried. They're soft, delicate, and very flavorful, but no longer juicy. Serve this silky pâté-style spread as a butter substitute. In flavor, it matches up well with almost any type of bread on the dinner table. As an appetizer spread, serve it on toasted onion baguette slices or bagel chips.

4 to 6 medium plum tomatoes, oven-dried (see Note)
1 tablespoon extra virgin olive oil
4 shallots, or 1/2 medium onion, finely chopped
2 cloves garlic, finely chopped
1 cup canned pinto beans, drained
1 tablespoon sugar
2 tablespoons fresh lemon juice
1 tablespoon white wine vinegar (preferably best quality)
2 teaspoons finely chopped fresh oregano, or 3/4 teaspoon dried
2 to 3 tablespoons finely chopped fresh basil
Salt
Freshly ground white pepper

1. Place the oven-dried tomatoes in the bowl of a food processor fitted with the metal blade. Pulse until coarsely chopped. Add 2 teaspoons of the olive oil and continue pulsing to a coarse purée.

2. Add the shallots or onion, garlic, beans, sugar, lemon juice, vinegar, oregano, basil, and remaining teaspoon of olive oil. Process to a smooth consistency. Add salt and white pepper to taste.

3. Transfer to a pâté dish or individual ramekins. Serve at room temperature or cover with plastic wrap, refrigerate, and serve chilled.

Note: To make oven-dried tomatoes, cut the tomatoes into 1 1/2-inch-thick slices, baste lightly with olive oil, and bake on parchment paper for 1 1/2 to 2 hours at 150°F.

Roasted Walnut, Lentil, and Mushroom Spread

Makes about 2 cups

1 cup tiny green Le Puy lentils (see page 60) or brown or red lentils
4 cups chicken or vegetable broth
$2^1/_2$ cups trimmed and thinly sliced mixed fresh mushrooms (about 1 pound), such as cremini, Portobello, and shiitake
2 cloves garlic, chopped
3 large shallots, chopped
2 tablespoons balsamic vinegar
$^1/_4$ cup plus 2 tablespoons extra virgin olive oil
Pinch of salt, or more to taste
Pinch of freshly ground black pepper, or more to taste
$1^1/_2$ cups toasted walnuts (see page xiv)
$^1/_2$ cup loosely packed chopped fresh basil, plus fresh basil leaves for garnish

Hearty and delicious, this vegetarian spread is also high in protein and very easy to make. Serve it with baked whole-wheat tortilla chips, multi-grain pita bread, or crackers.

1. In a medium, heavy saucepan, combine the lentils and the chicken or vegetable broth. Simmer over low heat until tender, about 15 minutes for the Le Puy lentils, 30 minutes for brown or red lentils. Drain and cool.

2. Preheat the oven to 350°F.

3. In a roasting pan, combine the mushrooms, garlic, shallots, balsamic vinegar, 2 tablespoons of the olive oil, salt, and pepper and toss to mix well. Roast in a single layer for 15 minutes.

4. In the bowl of a food processor fitted with the metal blade, combine the cooked lentils, roasted mushroom mixture, walnuts, chopped basil, and remaining $^1/_4$ cup of olive oil. Process to a smooth consistency. Adjust the seasoning with salt and pepper.

5. Press into a crock or terrine. Serve at room temperature.

Provençal Tapenade Spread

Makes about 1 1/2 cups

Serve this with anything that pairs well with olives, such as hard-boiled eggs, baked potato, toast, even celery sticks or Belgian endive spears. Or serve with baguette croûtes or fresh, crusty bread.

1 cup Niçoise or other oil-cured black olives, pitted
6 flat anchovy fillets, drained and chopped
2 tablespoons capers, rinsed, drained, and coarsely chopped
2 cloves garlic, finely chopped
Juice of 1 lemon
4 to 6 tablespoons extra virgin olive oil

1. In the bowl of a food processor fitted with the metal blade, combine all the ingredients except the oil and process to form a paste.

2. With the motor running, slowly add just enough oil to form a spreadable consistency. Transfer to a serving dish and serve at room temperature, or store in a tightly covered container in the refrigerator.

Cheese Spreads

Cheese and Wine Spreads

The traditional cheese tray with accompanying spirits is great. But here's a different approach, which combines the two, offering the opportunity to create a cheese tray that's unique in flavor. Serve any of these spreads with crackers, plain croûtes, and toasted baguette rounds.

Brie and Brandy

Makes about 2 cups

1 pound French or domestic Brie cheese, rind trimmed (optional)
2 tablespoons brandy
$^1/_2$ cup (1 stick) unsalted butter, room temperature
1 scallion, white part only, or 1 shallot, finely chopped
Pinch of salt
Pinch of freshly ground white pepper
1 tablespoon finely chopped flat-leaf parsley

1. In the bowl of a food processor fitted with the metal blade, combine all ingredients and process to a smooth consistency.

2. Press into a crock or ramekin and sprinkle the top with chopped parsley. Serve at room temperature, or cover with plastic wrap, refrigerate, and serve chilled.

Cheddar and Beer

Makes about 2 cups

1 cup grated sharp cheddar cheese, room temperature
1 cup grated caraway cheddar cheese, room temperature
$1/_2$ cup cream cheese, regular or low-fat, at room temperature
$1/_4$ cup best-quality beer
2 teaspoons Dijon-style mustard
1 clove garlic, finely chopped
2 tablespoons finely chopped flat-leaf parsley
Pinch of salt
Pinch of freshly ground white pepper
Pinch of paprika for garnish

1. In the bowl of a food processor fitted with the metal blade, combine all ingredients. Process to a smooth consistency.

2. Press into a crock or ramekin and top with paprika. Serve at room temperature, or cover with plastic wrap, refrigerate, and serve chilled.

Variation

Cheddar and Vodka
Substitute 2 tablespoons vodka for the beer.

Roquefort and Madeira

Makes about 1 $1/2$ cups

1 pound Roquefort cheese, room temperature
3 tablespoons unsalted butter or cream cheese, room temperature
2 to 3 tablespoons Madeira, or to taste
Pinch of salt
Pinch of freshly ground white pepper

1. In the bowl of a food processor fitted with the metal blade, combine all ingredients and process to a smooth consistency.

2. Press into a crock or ramekin. Serve at room temperature, or cover with plastic wrap, refrigerate, and serve chilled.

Variation

Roquefort and Sauterne

Substitute sauterne for the Madeira.

St. André and Armagnac

Makes about 1 $1/2$ cups

1 $1/2$ pounds St. André (see Note) or other triple-cream blue cheese
2 tablespoons armagnac or cognac
Pinch of salt
Pinch of freshly ground white pepper

1. In the bowl of a food processor fitted with the metal blade, combine all ingredients. Process to a smooth consistency.

2. Press into a crock or ramekin. Serve at room temperature.

Note: St. André is a triple-cream blue cheese that is very rich and mild.

Chèvre and Chardonnay

Makes 2 cups

1¹/₂ cups fresh fromage blanc (see Note) or ricotta, well drained
3 tablespoons extra virgin olive oil
¹/₃ cup chardonnay or other dry white wine
²/₃ cup heavy cream, chilled
2 shallots, finely chopped
¹/₃ cup finely chopped flat-leaf parsley
2 tablespoons chopped fresh chives
2 tablespoons chopped fresh chervil
Salt
Freshly ground black pepper

1. In a small bowl, place the cheese and mash with a fork. Add the olive oil and wine and stir until well combined.

2. In another bowl, whip the cream until stiff. Fold a bit of the whipped cream into the cheese mixture, then fold the cheese into the cream. Add the shallots, parsley, chives, and chervil and stir to mix. Season to taste with salt and pepper.

3. Transfer to a serving bowl, cover with plastic wrap, and refrigerate. Serve chilled.

Note: Fromage blanc is fresh, unaged goat cheese. Buy it by the pound, as you would yogurt, in cheese shops or gourmet grocery stores. Or use Montrachet.

Gorgonzola and Grappa

Makes about 1 1/4 cups

1/2 pound gorgonzola cheese, at room temperature
1/2 cup low-fat cream cheese
2 tablespoons sour cream, regular or low-fat
2 to 3 tablespoons grappa, or to taste
Pinch of salt
Pinch of freshly ground white pepper

1. In the bowl of a food processor fitted with the metal blade, combine all ingredients and process to a smooth consistency.

2. Press into a crock or serving bowl and serve at room temperature, or cover with plastic wrap, refrigerate, and serve chilled.

Stilton and Scotch

Makes about 1 1/2 cups

1 1/2 pounds English Stilton cheese, crumbled
3 tablespoons unsalted butter, room temperature
2 to 3 tablespoons Scotch
1 shallot, finely chopped (optional)
Pinch of freshly ground black pepper
Cracked black peppercorns for garnish

1. In the bowl of a food processor fitted with the metal blade, combine the Stilton, butter, Scotch, shallot, if using, and pepper. Process to a smooth consistency.

2. Press into a crock or serving dish and top with a scant amount of cracked peppercorns. Serve at room temperature.

Variation

Stilton and Port

Substitute port for the Scotch.

Aged Chèvre and Vermouth

Makes about 2 cups

¹/₂ cup dry vermouth or dry white wine
¹/₂ cup defatted chicken broth
2 tablespoons Dijon-style mustard
2 tablespoons unsalted butter
3 shallots, finely chopped
¹/₄ cup loosely packed finely chopped flat-leaf parsley
12 ounces aged chèvre (see page 23), crumbled
¹/₄ cup low-fat cream cheese, room temperature, fluffed with a fork
Salt
Freshly ground black pepper

1. In a small, heavy saucepan, combine the vermouth and chicken broth. Bring to a boil and reduce until about 2 tablespoons remain. Stir in the mustard, transfer to a bowl, and set aside to cool to room temperature.

2. In the same saucepan, melt the butter. Add the shallots and cook until tender. Combine with the vermouth and mustard mixture.

3. In the bowl of a food processor fitted with the metal blade, combine the vermouth mixture, parsley, chèvre, and cream cheese and process to a smooth consistency. Season to taste with salt and pepper.

4. Press into a crock or ramekin and serve at room temperature. Or cover with plastic wrap, refrigerate, and serve chilled.

Sun-Dried Tomato and Cream Cheese Spread

Makes 1 1/2 cups

10 medium dry-packed sun-dried tomato halves, softened for 30 minutes in very hot water, broth, or wine, or 10 medium oil-packed sun-dried tomato halves

1 pound (16 ounces) cream cheese, nonfat, low-fat, or regular, at room temperature

3 or more turns of the peppermill

1. Drain the sun-dried tomato halves slightly. Or, if desired, pat off excess oil with paper towels. Chop coarsely.

2. On a shallow round or oval serving dish, mound the cream cheese in large spoonfuls.

3. Sprinkle the tomato pieces over the cream cheese. Press the tomatoes down into the cheese but do not stir. Top with a few turns of the peppermill. Serve at room temperature.

Serve this rich and creamy-tasting, yet fat-conscious spread with a loaf of hot, crusty country bread. The taste of the nonfat cream cheese is every bit as delicious as regular cream cheese when served this way.

Garlic and Herb Cheese Spread

Makes about 1 cup

Serve this low-fat spread with fat-free crackers, cracked-wheat crackers, rice cakes, or fresh vegetable slices.

8 ounces cream cheese, low-fat or nonfat
$1/2$ cup sour cream, low-fat or nonfat
2 tablespoons nonfat yogurt
1 tablespoon Roasted Garlic Purée (page 3) or 1 large clove garlic,
    finely chopped and sautéed gently in $1/8$ teaspoon olive oil until soft
1 tablespoon finely chopped fresh chives
2 teaspoons finely chopped fresh basil
1 tablespoon chopped flat-leaf parsley
Salt
Freshly ground black pepper

1. In the bowl of a food processor fitted with the metal blade, combine all of the ingredients and process to a smooth consistency. Season to taste with salt and pepper.

2. Transfer to a small serving bowl. Serve at room temperature, or cover with plastic wrap, refrigerate, and serve chilled.

Hungarian-Style Goat Cheese Spread

Makes about 1 cup

8 ounces aged chèvre (see below), rind removed
$1/2$ cup (1 stick) unsalted butter, room temperature
$1^1/_2$ tablespoons chopped fresh chives
2 teaspoons anchovy paste (optional)
1 teaspoon small capers, rinsed, drained, and finely chopped
1 teaspoon Dijon-style or grainy mustard
$1/2$ teaspoon ground caraway seeds
$1/2$ teaspoon hot paprika, plus a pinch for garnish
1 teaspoon finely chopped flat-leaf parsley for garnish

1. In the bowl of a food processor fitted with the metal blade, combine all the ingredients except the parsley and process to a smooth consistency.

2. Transfer to a small bowl, cover with plastic wrap, and refrigerate 4 hours to marinate.

3. Transfer to a crock or serving dish and sprinkle the top with a pinch of paprika and the parsley. Chill for 30 minutes before serving.

Chèvre or Goat Cheese?

Although we call it just plain old goat cheese, the French call it chèvre and have many names for the different shapes and sizes of goat cheese pieces to indicate the age or freshness of this tangy, soft cheese. There are many imported and domestic variations available for both aged and fresh goat cheese, each with a distinctly different tang to the flavor. It is best to experiment and use the ones you prefer.

Serve this traditional spread with celery stalks, dark bread with raisins, rye or pumpernickel bread, dark wheat crackers, or breadsticks. For the chèvre, choose a crottin (shaped like a patty) or other chèvre aged 2 to 3 weeks.

Goat Cheese and Chutney Spread

Makes about 1 cup

Serve with crackers or croûtes, fresh baguette slices, or a variety of vegetables slices.

5 to 7 ounces fresh chèvre (see page 23), such as Montrachet, room
    temperature
$3/4$ cup sweet or savory chutney, such as apple, strawberry, tomato, onion
    (see pages 57, 58, 86, 106, 107)

1. Place the cheese in a mixing bowl. Stir in the chutney until well combined. Transfer to a serving dish.

2. Cover with plastic wrap, refrigerate, and serve chilled.

Broiled Black Pepper Chèvre Spread

Makes about $3/4$ cup

This peppery, hot spread is a great match with garlic croûtes, a warmed whole loaf of bread, or even raw vegetable slices.

1 tablespoon extra virgin olive oil
Pinch of cayenne pepper
7 to 12 ounces fresh chèvre (see page 23)
10 turns of the peppermill, or more to taste

1. Preheat the broiler.

2. In a small bowl, combine the oil and cayenne. In a separate bowl, combine the cheese and half the oil mixture. Line a small bowl with plastic wrap. Press the goat cheese in the bottom of the bowl to form an upside-down dome.

3. Turn the mold out onto a flameproof baking dish lined with aluminum foil. Brush on the remaining oil mixture. Top with 10 turns of the peppermill, or more if desired. Broil placed as far from the flame as possible, until warm throughout and a golden crust forms, about 5 minutes. Do not burn.

4. Transfer to a serving plate and serve immediately.

Warm Spinach, Parsley, and Goat Cheese Spread

Makes about 1 cup

1/2 cup water
1 pound fresh spinach, washed well and stemmed (see Note)
1 tablespoon extra virgin olive oil
1 tablespoon unsalted butter
2 tablespoons all-purpose flour
2 large cloves garlic, pressed
1/4 cup finely chopped flat-leaf parsley
5 to 7 ounces chèvre, aged or fresh (see page 23), rind removed if necessary,
    cut into pieces
Salt
Freshly ground black pepper

Serve this with crisp sesame crackers.

1. In a medium skillet, heat 1/2 cup water to very hot. Reduce the heat to very very low and wilt the spinach for 1 minute. Drain the spinach, reserving the cooking liquid, and pat dry on paper towels. Chop and set aside.

2. In a medium, heavy skillet or sauté pan, heat the olive oil and butter together over medium-high heat. Sprinkle the flour into the pan, reduce the heat to low, and cook 4 to 5 minutes, stirring constantly with a wooden spoon. Do not allow the flour to brown.

3. Add the garlic and continue to cook about 1 minute more. Turn the heat to medium and slowly begin adding the reserved spinach liquid. Continue cooking until all the liquid is absorbed into the flour mixture. Continue adding up to 1/4 cup more of the reserved liquid or water until the mixture is smooth.

4. Stir in the spinach, lower the heat to very low, and cook, partially covered, 5 minutes more. Remove the skillet from the heat and stir in the parsley and cheese just to mix. Season to taste with salt and pepper. Transfer to a serving bowl and serve immediately.

Note: Substitute one 10-ounce package of frozen chopped spinach, thawed in a colander, reserving the liquid, and pressed to remove any moisture.

Wine-Drenched Coeur à la Crème
(Savory or Sweet)

Makes about one 6-cup mold

Perfect for special occasion entertaining, this elegant spread molded into the shape of a heart is a classic in France, where it is often served at weddings. Translated, coeur à la crème means "heart of cream." The process involved is quite a bit more time-consuming than the other spreads in this book, but the results are both rewarding and delicious. Serve it with delicate water crackers.

4 cups plain yogurt, regular or low-fat
$1/2$ cup wine of choice, such as port, red or white wine, or champagne
1 cup cream cheese, regular or low-fat, at room temperature
$1/4$ cup dry red or white wine or brut champagne, chilled
1 envelope unflavored gelatin

For Savory

2 tablespoons finely chopped yellow onion
$1/2$ cup finely chopped mixed fresh herbs, such as chives, basil, and flat-leaf parsley
$1/2$ teaspoon salt
$1/4$ teaspoon freshly ground white pepper
Fresh leaves for garnish, such as chives, basil, or flat-leaf parsley

For Sweet

2 teaspoons grated lemon zest
$1/4$ cup sugar dissolved in 2 teaspoons lemon juice, or 3 tablespoons orange juice concentrate
Fresh leaves for garnish, such as mint leaves or edible flowers

1. Line a colander with 4 layers of cheesecloth, allowing the excess to hang over the edge, and place over a large bowl. Spoon in the yogurt. Cover loosely with plastic wrap and refrigerate 12 hours to drain. Transfer the yogurt into a clean bowl and discard the cheesecloth and liquid. Set aside.

2. Soak another 3 layers of cheesecloth in the $1/2$ cup wine of choice for 30 seconds. Squeeze out the excess so the cheesecloth is barely damp, reserving 2 tablespoons of the wine if making the sweet version. Line a 4-cup heart-shaped mold or other shaped mold with the wine-dampened cheesecloth, allowing the excess cheesecloth to hang over the edge, and set aside.

3. For savory: In the bowl of a food processor fitted with the metal blade, combine the onion, chopped herbs, salt, pepper, and cream cheese. Process to a smooth consistency. Stir in the drained yogurt and set aside.

For sweet: In the bowl of a food processor fitted with the metal blade, combine the reserved 2 tablespoons of wine (from step 2), lemon zest, sugar mixture, and cream cheese. Process to a smooth consistency. Stir in the drained yogurt and set aside.

4. In a small saucepan, place the chilled $1/4$ cup wine or champagne. Sprinkle with the gelatin and let stand 1 minute. Cook over low heat, stirring, until the gelatin dissolves. Remove from the heat, place in a shallow bowl in the refrigerator for about 30 minutes, and let cool and thicken slightly, but do not let the gelatin set. Whisk 2 tablespoons of the yogurt mixture into the gelatin. Then add the gelatin mixture to the remaining yogurt mixture, stirring gently to blend.

5. Spoon the yogurt–gelatin mixture into the prepared mold and tap the bottom on a hard surface. Fold the cheesecloth over the top and refrigerate for 12 hours. To unmold, gently unfold the cheesecloth and invert the mold onto a serving plate. Garnish with fresh leaves.

For recipes calling for this Spread, see pages 34, 67, and 77.

Yogurt Cheese

Makes 1 cup

Serve yogurt cheese as a low-fat substitute for a regular semisoft cheese such as chèvre or Brie. A variety of flavorings—herbs and spices, vegetable or fruit purées, roasted garlic, and chopped tomatoes—can be added after yogurt is drained to make a spread. And many recipes in this book call for yogurt cheese as an ingredient. It's even suitable for dessert cheese spreads when served with sweet crackers.

2 cups plain yogurt, nonfat or low-fat

1. Line a colander with 4 layers of cheesecloth. Place the colander in a bowl.

2. Spoon in the yogurt and let drain for 2 to 6 hours. The longer the yogurt drains, the more dense the cheese will be.

Variations

Yogurt Cheese with Herb and Roasted Garlic

After the yogurt drains for 2 to 4 hours, transfer to a bowl. Mix in finely chopped fresh herbs, salt and pepper to taste, and Roasted Garlic Purée (page 3) to taste.

Yogurt Cheese Ball

Line the colander with a piece of porous cloth, such as muslin, large enough to cover the yogurt and tie the ends together at the top. Spoon the yogurt into the colander and drain over a bowl. After about 2 hours, draw the ends of the cloth together, forming the yogurt into a ball. Tie tightly with kitchen string. Hang the ball by the string and allow to drain over a bowl up to 24 hours in the refrigerator. Serve as a cheese. Flavorings like finely chopped fresh vegetables (radishes, celery, carrots), chopped dried fruits and nuts, or spices and condiments may be added after the yogurt drains for 2 hours.

Lemony Feta Spread

Makes about 1 1/2 cups

1/2 cup cream cheese, regular, low-fat, or nonfat
12 ounces feta cheese, drained and crumbled
Grated zest of 1 lemon
2 large shallots, finely chopped
1 teaspoon fresh lemon juice
1 tablespoon finely chopped fresh herbs, such as oregano, cilantro, parsley,
   or dill
Freshly ground white pepper

1. In the bowl of a food processor fitted with the metal blade, combine all the ingredients except the pepper and process to a smooth consistency. Season to taste with white pepper.

2. Transfer to a serving bowl and serve immediately. Or cover with plastic wrap, refrigerate, and serve chilled.

It's Greek to Me

Although feta began in Greece as a firm sheep's milk cheese, the domestic version, made of cow's milk, is great for this spread.

Serve this tangy cheese spread with an assortment of crisp fresh vegetables and breads, along with Cucumber and Yogurt Topper (page 77).

Bell Pepper Mayonnaise

Makes about 2 cups

This versatile spread can be used anywhere mayo is called for, especially as a sandwich spread. But it is also great in chicken or fish salads.

2 yellow or red bell peppers, roasted, peeled, and seeded (see page xiv), and cut into strips
2 large egg yolks
2 to 4 cloves garlic, finely chopped
$^3/_4$ to 1 cup extra virgin olive oil or canola oil
Salt
Freshly ground white pepper

1. In the bowl of a food processor fitted with the metal blade, process the peppers to a smooth purée. Transfer to a colander lined with a double layer of cheesecloth or to a fine-mesh strainer, and let sit over a bowl to drain for 1 hour.

2. In the clean bowl of a food processor fitted with the metal blade, combine the egg yolks and garlic. Process until well combined. With the motor running, add a few drops of oil at a time, incorporating each addition completely before adding more. When the mixture begins to mount up, pour in the olive oil in a thin but steady stream. From this point, add only enough oil to make a light and fluffy mayonnaise. (You may not need to use all of the oil.)

3. Stir in the drained pepper purée. Season to taste with salt and pepper. Transfer to a serving bowl or refrigerate in a tightly covered jar until ready to use.

Vegetable Spreads

Fresh Mushroom Spread

Makes about 1 1/2 cups

1 pound fresh mushrooms, such as porcini, oyster, chanterelle, or cultivated
    white, well washed, trimmed, dried, and roughly chopped
1 clove garlic, pressed
2 tablespoons fresh lemon juice
1/4 cup extra virgin olive oil
1 tablespoon balsamic vinegar
1 bunch chives, finely chopped, or 1/4 cup finely chopped scallion,
    green part only
Salt
Freshly ground black pepper

Serve this deep-flavored spread with herb croûtes, crackers, or potato wedges.

1. In the bowl of a food processor fitted with the metal blade, process the mushrooms and garlic to a very coarse consistency.

2. Add the lemon juice, olive oil, and balsamic vinegar. Process to a smoother consistency with some texture remaining. Stir in the chives. Season with salt and pepper to taste.

3. Press into a crock or terrine and serve at room temperature.

Avocado Spread

Makes about 1 1/2 cups

Think of this as faux mayo! Use it as a sandwich spread instead of mayonnaise, or instead of butter or oil on bruschetta—then top with your favorite ingredients.

2 medium ripe Haas avocados, halved, pitted, and flesh scooped out
2 cloves garlic, pressed
4 scallions, white and some green parts, finely chopped
2 tablespoons finely chopped flat-leaf parsley or cilantro
Juice of 1 lime or lemon
1/2 small jalapeño chile, deveined, seeded, and finely chopped (see page xiv)
1/2 cup canola oil
Salt
Freshly ground white pepper

1. In the bowl of a food processor fitted with the metal blade, combine the avocado, garlic, scallions, 1 tablespoon of the parsley or cilantro, half the lemon or lime juice, and the jalapeño. Process to a smooth consistency.

2. With the motor running, add the oil in a thin but steady stream until completely incorporated into the avocado mixture. Add the remaining lemon or lime juice and pulse just to mix. Season to taste with salt and white pepper.

3. Transfer to a serving bowl. Sprinkle with the remaining tablespoon of parsley or cilantro. Serve at room temperature, or cover with plastic wrap, making sure the wrap is touching the top of the spread to prevent air from turning it dark. Store in the refrigerator until ready to serve.

Fresh from the Mill

The peppermill is essential for making delicious spreads, toppers, and dips. Because the flavor of pepper subsides very quickly after being ground, it is best to grind it seconds before using and to add it as a final ingredient.

It's almost a necessity to have two peppermills handy—one with black peppercorns and one with white peppercorns. As a rule, use black pepper when making dark-colored spreads, toppers, and dips, and white pepper when making recipes that are light in color. Although the peppers taste the same, your finished product will have a more agreeable appearance.

Parsley, Leek, and Fennel Spread

Makes about 2¹/₂ cups

Serve this sautéed vegetable spread with herb toast or homemade Goat Cheese Crackers (page 167) or as an accompaniment to a grilled vegetable platter. To make this spread thick and creamy, see the Variations.

3 tablespoons unsalted butter
2 medium leeks, white part only, leaves separated and thoroughly cleaned, then thinly sliced
1 medium fennel bulb, bottom and top trimmed, thinly sliced
¹/₂ cup finely chopped flat-leaf parsley
1 tablespoon fresh lemon juice
2 tablespoons dry white wine
Pinch of cayenne pepper
Salt
Freshly ground black pepper

1. In a medium, heavy skillet melt the butter over medium heat. Add the leeks and fennel and cook, partially covered, over low heat, stirring frequently, until the vegetables are very tender and soft, about 30 minutes.

2. Remove from the heat and stir in the parsley, lemon juice, wine, and cayenne. Transfer to the bowl of a food processor fitted with the metal blade. Pulse several times to process to a smooth consistency. Season to taste with salt and pepper.

3. Transfer to a serving bowl and serve warm. Or cover with plastic wrap and refrigerate until ready to serve. Rewarm before serving.

Variations

For a thick and creamy version, add ¹/₂ cup riced or diced cooked potato to the processor at the end, along with ¹/₄ cup well-drained ricotta or Yogurt Cheese (page 28). Do not reheat.

Endive and Chervil Spread

Substitute 3 to 4 Belgian endive bulbs for the leeks, and fresh chopped chervil for the parsley. (Can also be made thick and creamy as in above variation.)

Moroccan Carrot Spread

Makes about 2 cups

1 pound carrots, peeled, cut in half lengthwise, then across into 1-inch-long
   pieces
2^1/$_2$ tablespoons extra virgin olive oil
2 tablespoons red wine vinegar
1 clove garlic, pressed
^{3}/$_4$ teaspoon ground cumin
^{3}/$_4$ teaspoon sweet paprika
^{1}/$_4$ teaspoon salt
^{1}/$_4$ teaspoon freshly ground black pepper

1. In a vegetable steamer, cook the carrots just until done but still slightly crunchy, about 10 minutes.

2. Place the carrots in the bowl of a food processor fitted with the metal blade. Process to a coarse purée. Transfer to a mixing bowl.

3. Add the remaining ingredients and stir to mix well.

4. Transfer to a serving dish and serve immediately, or cover with plastic wrap and chill well before serving.

Serve this colorful and tasty spread on Herb or Spice Pita Chips (page 162) or another flatbread. Recipe maven Rozanne Gold of New York City created the recipe one summer day, but she says it's great all year round, too.

Sautéed Spinach Spread

Makes about 2 cups

Serve this rich, smooth, and creamy spread instead of butter. Crunchy seeded hearth-baked breads and crackers are perfect accompaniments. Try this recipe using broccoli florets instead of spinach for a delicious change.

1¹/₂ cups canned white beans (Great Northern) or chickpeas (garbanzo beans), rinsed and well drained
2 tablespoons fresh lemon juice
2 tablespoons water
2 teaspoons small capers, rinsed and drained, or 2 teaspoons grated lemon zest
¹/₄ cup extra virgin olive oil
2 large cloves garlic, finely chopped
8 cups loosely packed spinach, stemmed, washed, dried, and roughly chopped, or one (10-ounce) package frozen chopped spinach, thawed, drained in a colander, excess moisture pressed out
Freshly ground black pepper
Salt

1. In the bowl of a food processor fitted with the metal blade, combine the beans, 1 tablespoon of the lemon juice, the water, the capers or lemon zest, and 2 tablespoons of the olive oil. Process to a smooth consistency. Transfer to a mixing bowl and set aside.

2. In a large skillet, heat the remaining oil over medium heat. Add the garlic and cook for 1 minute. Add the spinach, cover the pan, and cook for about 1 minute. Remove the skillet from the heat and stir in pepper to taste and the remaining tablespoon of lemon juice.

3. Stir the spinach into the bean mixture. Season to taste with salt and pepper.

4. Transfer to a serving dish and serve at room temperature.

Ginger Yam and Sweet Potato Spread

Makes about 1 1/4 cups

1 large yam (red if available), about 3/4 pound, well scrubbed
1 large sweet potato, about 3/4 pound, well scrubbed
3/4 teaspoon grated fresh ginger
2 tablespoons fresh lime juice
2 teaspoons grated lime zest
1 tablespoon unsalted butter, melted
1 tablespoon tahini, or more to taste
1 tablespoon sour cream, regular or low-fat
Salt
Freshly ground white pepper
2 tablespoons finely chopped golden raisins
2 tablespoons coarsely chopped toasted pecans or walnuts (see page xiv)

1. Preheat the oven to 350°F.

2. Place the yam and sweet potato on a baking sheet lined with aluminum foil. Bake until tender throughout, 1 to 1 1/2 hours.

3. When cool enough to handle, peel the potatoes and place in the bowl of a food processor fitted with the metal blade. Add the ginger, lime juice and zest, butter, tahini, and sour cream. Process to a smooth spread, leaving some texture if desired. Season to taste with salt and pepper. Stir in the raisins and nuts.

4. Transfer to a serving dish. Serve warm or at room temperature.

Serve this colorful spread heaped in a bowl beside a basket of whole-grain dark bread. It is a wonderful alternative to butter and a great deal tastier.

Chunky Artichoke Spread

Makes about 2 cups

Serve this spread with crisp whole-wheat crackers, pretzel sticks, seeded breadsticks, croûtes, or melbas.

One 12-ounce bag frozen artichoke hearts (or bottoms with heart portion),
    thawed, stems trimmed, and coarsely chopped
1 tablespoon canola oil
$^1/_4$ cup sour cream, regular, low-fat, or nonfat
1 clove garlic, finely chopped
1 teaspoon grated lemon zest
$^1/_4$ teaspoon salt
$^1/_4$ teaspoon freshly ground white pepper
2 to 4 turns of the peppermill

1. Place the chopped artichoke hearts in a strainer and press with the back of a wooden spoon to extract as much of the liquid as possible. Spread out on a cutting board and pat dry with paper towels.

2. In a medium, heavy skillet or sauté pan, heat the oil over medium heat. Add the artichoke hearts and cook, stirring occasionally, until tender and all the moisture has evaporated, 5 to 7 minutes. Let cool to room temperature.

3. In the bowl of a food processor fitted with the metal blade, combine the artichoke hearts, sour cream, garlic, lemon zest, salt, and white pepper. Process to a spreadable consistency. Some texture will remain.

4. Transfer to a serving bowl, top with a few turns of the peppermill, and serve at room temperature.

Curried Squash Spread

Makes 1 1/8 cups

1 large butternut or acorn squash (about 1¼ pounds)
1½ tablespoons unsalted butter
3 medium shallots, finely chopped
½ teaspoon mild or hot curry powder (Madras or best quality available),
    or to taste
1 teaspoon pure maple syrup or honey
Salt
Freshly ground black pepper

1. Preheat the oven to 450°F. Line a baking sheet with aluminum foil.

2. Cut the squash in half lengthwise and scoop out the seeds and discard. Place the squash, cut side down, on the foil and bake until tender throughout, about ½ hour. When cool enough to handle, scoop out the flesh into a fine-mesh strainer to drain.

3. In a medium, heavy skillet or sauté pan, melt the butter over medium heat. Add the shallots and curry powder and cook until the shallots are tender, 3 to 4 minutes. Add the squash, maple syrup or honey, and salt and pepper to taste. Mash the squash and continue cooking, stirring and mashing, until the moisture has evaporated, 5 to 6 minutes.

4. Transfer to the bowl of a food processor fitted with the metal blade. Process to a smooth pureé.

5. Transfer to a serving bowl. Serve at room temperature.

For a trio of fresh-flavored low-fat spreads for hors d'oeuvres, accompany this spread with Sautéed Spinach Spread (page 36) and White Bean Mousse (page 61). Thinly sliced pumpernickel is a perfect match. Or serve this bright yellow spread instead of butter with a basket of various breads.

Fresh Greens Spread

Makes about 1 cup

Serve this fresh, delicious spread with anything that is fairly bland in flavor, such as potatoes or freshly fried Homemade Vegetable Chips (page 168). As a vegetarian spread, this is a great choice.

1½ tablespoons unsalted butter
4 medium shallots, finely chopped
½ pound fresh spinach, stemmed, washed well, and patted dry with paper towels
½ cup watercress, leaves only
¼ cup finely chopped flat-leaf parsley
⅓ cup half-and-half
1 tablespoon sour cream, regular or low-fat
Salt
Freshly ground black pepper

1. In a large skillet or sauté pan, melt the butter over medium heat. Add the shallots and cook until tender. Add the spinach and watercress, cover, and cook over low heat just until wilted, 2 to 3 minutes, turning once during cooking.

2. Add the parsley and half-and-half. Increase the heat to medium-high and cook, stirring frequently, until the mixture thickens and the half-and-half is completely absorbed, about 6 minutes.

3. Transfer the mixture to the bowl of a food processor fitted with the metal blade. Add the sour cream and pulse 4 to 5 times to form a smooth consistency. Season to taste with salt and pepper.

4. Transfer to a serving bowl and serve warm.

Two-Minute Smoked Salmon Spread

Makes about $1^1/_2$ cups

$^3/_4$ pound smoked salmon, chopped
$^1/_3$ cup plain yogurt, regular, low-fat, or nonfat
Pinch of freshly ground white pepper
$^1/_4$ teaspoon sweet or hot paprika (optional)
$^1/_2$ tablespoon extra virgin olive oil
2 teaspoons grated lemon zest
2 tablespoons fresh lemon juice
2 tablespoons finely chopped scallion, white and green parts chopped
   separately

1. In the bowl of a food processor fitted with the metal blade, combine half of the salmon with the remaining ingredients except the scallion. Process to a smooth purée.

2. Stir in the remaining salmon and the white part of the scallion.

3. Transfer to a serving dish, cover with plastic wrap, and chill for 30 minutes. Sprinkle with the green scallion before serving.

Serve this quick-to-make but delicious spread with country-style breads, coarse dark bread, crumpets, or blini.

Anchovy, Egg, and Aquavit Spread

Makes about 1 1/2 cups

Aquavit is the liqueur of choice in the midst of a frigid Scandinavian winter. Here, a few drops hint of the taste of an extract. Serve this with thinly sliced, strong-flavored dark breads, such as pumpernickel or rye toast. It's also a perfect spread for blinis, or try it on vegetable rounds, such as cucumber, squash, or yellow beets, for a unique Norse-influenced combination.

8 hard-boiled eggs, peeled
6 to 8 flat anchovy fillets, drained and finely chopped
1/3 cup cream cheese, regular or low-fat
1 tablespoon extra virgin olive oil
1 to 2 tablespoons regular or caraway aquavit, or more to taste
Grated zest of 1 lemon, or 1 tablespoon rinsed and drained small capers
Pinch of freshly ground white pepper

1. With a fine steel grater, grate the egg yolks and whites separately.

2. In the bowl of a food processor fitted with the metal blade, combine the grated egg yolks, anchovies, and cream cheese. Pulse a few times to blend well. Pour in the olive oil and aquavit 1 tablespoon at a time, pulsing to incorporate between additions.

3. Add the lemon zest or capers and the white pepper to taste, and pulse just to mix. Transfer the mixture to a medium mixing bowl, add the grated egg whites, and stir gently until well blended.

4. Transfer to a serving crock or bowl. Serve at room temperature or chill before serving.

Tuna Pâté

Makes about 1 cup

One 6-ounce can oil- or water-packed dark tuna, drained and moisture
   pressed out
$^1/_4$ cup ($^1/_2$ stick) unsalted butter, room temperature
2 tablespoons chopped flat-leaf parsley
1 tablespoon finely chopped white onion
1 teaspoon fresh lemon juice
$^1/_2$ teaspoon grated lemon zest
Freshly ground white pepper

1. In a medium mixing bowl, place the tuna and break apart the pieces with a fork.

2. Mash in the butter, all but 1 teaspoon of the parsley, and the onion, lemon juice, and zest. Mash together with a fork until well combined. Season to taste with white pepper.

3. Press into a terrine or ramekin. Sprinkle with the remaining 1 teaspoon parsley. Cover with plastic wrap, refrigerate, and serve chilled.

Variation

Classic Tuna Spread

Instead of the butter, use mayonnaise, and substitute 1 to 2 chopped scallions for the white onion. (To save some calories, choose water-packed tuna and use reduced-fat mayonnaise.)

Serve this unadulterated and delicious spread with melba toast, pumpernickel, or crisp wheat crackers—even on Ritz!

Golden Caviar Spread

Makes about 2 cups

If Beluga seems a bit pricey and Osetra a bit salty for your taste, this is a light and tasty alternative. Golden caviar, which comes from whitefish, is exceptionally priced at about $14 for the 4 ounces called for in this recipe. It's best when purchased from a fish market. This is definitely caviar at its best! Serve with delicate blinis or tiny crumpets.

1 cup crème fraîche (see Note)
3 scallions, white and some green parts, finely chopped
Grated zest of 1 lemon
Juice of 1 lemon, or to taste
$2/_3$ cup fresh bread crumbs
Pinch of cayenne pepper
2 teaspoons extra virgin olive oil
3 to 4 ounces (about $3/_4$ cup) whitefish caviar (golden eggs)
2 tablespoons chopped fresh chives for garnish

1. In the bowl of a food processor fitted with the metal blade, combine the crème fraîche, scallions, lemon zest and juice, bread crumbs, and cayenne and pulse to a smooth consistency. With the motor running, add the oil a few drops at a time until completely incorporated.

2. Transfer to a serving bowl, fold in the caviar, and garnish with chives. Serve immediately.

Note: Crème fraîche is a thick, cultured cream. It makes a great addition to spreads and dips and is a versatile cooking ingredient. If it is unavailable in your supermarket, simply make your own. Mix $2^1/_2$ cups heavy cream with 2 tablespoons buttermilk and let stand for 3 to 4 hours in a warm (75° to 80°F) area on or near the stove. Stir and refrigerate.

Variation

Red Caviar Spread

Instead of whitefish caviar, use salmon caviar. (Price is about $24 for 4 ounces.)

Chicken Liver and Hazelnut Pâté

Makes about 1 1/2 cups

2 cups water
1/2 pound chicken livers (choose lighter-colored livers if possible), rinsed, dried, and trimmed of membranes, veins, and spots
6 tablespoons (3/4 stick) unsalted butter
1 small onion, chopped
1 clove garlic, chopped
2 tablespoons cognac
2 tablespoons heavy cream or crème fraîche
Salt
Freshly ground white pepper
1/2 cup plus 2 tablespoons chopped toasted hazelnuts, skins rubbed off (see page xiv)

This classic pâté will be a welcome addition to the buffet table at both casual and formal affairs.

1. In a medium saucepan, bring the water to a boil. Add the livers, reduce the heat to low, cover, and cook for 5 minutes. Drain and set aside.

2. In a medium, heavy skillet or sauté pan, melt 3 tablespoons butter over medium–low heat. Add onion and garlic and cook until translucent. Add livers, stir, and continue cooking until done throughout, about 3 minutes more. Let cool slightly.

3. In the bowl of a food processor fitted with the metal blade, process the liver mixture to a smooth spread. Melt the remaining 3 tablespoons of butter and add to the liver spread, along with the cognac and cream or crème fraîche. Process until well blended. Add salt and white pepper to taste. Stir in 1/2 cup hazelnuts.

4. Transfer the spread to a terrine or individual ramekins. Cover with plastic wrap and refrigerate. Let stand at room temperature for 30 minutes before serving, and top with the remaining hazelnuts.

Mango Chicken Spread

Makes about 2 cups

Serve this spread on toasted whole-grain bread or on vegetable or bread canapés. For variety, substitute a different flavor for the mango chutney, such as peach or onion and apple (both chutneys are commercially made). Or choose one of the chutney recipes in this book (see pages 57, 58, 86, 106, 107).

2$^1/_2$ cups defatted chicken broth
4 skinless, boneless chicken breast halves (about 1$^1/_2$ pounds trimmed)
$^1/_3$ cup mayonnaise, regular or low-fat
$^1/_4$ cup chopped mango chutney
Salt
Freshly ground white pepper

1. In a medium skillet, bring the chicken broth to a simmer. Add the chicken breasts and poach, uncovered, just until done throughout, about 8 minutes. Let cool to room temperature in the poaching liquid. Coarsely chop the chicken and transfer to the bowl of a food processor fitted with the metal blade.

2. Process the chicken breast pieces to a coarse pâté. Add the mayonnaise and chutney and process until smooth. Season to taste with salt and white pepper.

3. Transfer to a serving bowl or terrine. Serve at room temperature, or cover with plastic wrap, refrigerate, and serve chilled.

Honey-Baked Ham and Cheddar Spread

Makes about 3 cups

2 cups coarsely chopped honey-baked or smoked ham
1 cup grated sharp cheddar cheese
1/4 cup chopped flat-leaf parsley
2 scallions, white and some green parts, chopped
1/2 teaspoon ground caraway seed
1 teaspoon dried dill
3/4 cup mayonnaise, regular or low-fat
1/4 cup cream cheese, regular or low-fat, at room temperature
1 to 2 tablespoons dry white vermouth or fresh lemon juice
1 to 2 teaspoons grainy or Dijon-style mustard
Salt
Freshly ground white pepper
1 tablespoon chopped fresh dill for garnish

Surround a crock of this well-loved combination of flavors with crisp crackers, such as homemade Polenta Crisps (page 169).

1. In the bowl of a food processor fitted with the metal blade, combine the ham, cheddar cheese, parsley, scallions, ground caraway seed, and dried dill. Process by pulsing to form a coarse pâté.

2. In a small bowl, combine the mayonnaise, cream cheese, vermouth or lemon juice, and mustard. Stir to mix. Add to the ham mixture and pulse to mix well. Season to taste with salt and white pepper.

3. Transfer to a terrine or crock, sprinkle with the fresh dill, and serve at room temperature. Or cover with plastic wrap and chill before serving.

Variation

Reuben and Swiss Spread

Substitute chopped corned beef for the ham and best-quality Swiss cheese for the cheddar. Add 1 cup well-drained sauerkraut to the food processor and use finely chopped white onion or shallots instead of the scallion.

Coconut and Strawberry Spread

Makes about 1 1/2 cups

Serve this slightly sweet, ambrosia-like spread on warm fruit bread, such as raisin pumpernickel or date-nut. It is perfect as an accompaniment to tea or coffee, especially in the afternoon.

2 tablespoons sour cream, regular or low-fat
1 cup cream cheese, regular or low-fat
1/8 teaspoon vanilla extract, or 1 teaspoon brandy
Pinch of sugar
1/3 cup shredded unsweetened coconut, toasted (see Note)
1/2 cup sliced fresh strawberries
3 tablespoons chopped toasted hazelnuts, skins rubbed off (see page xiv)

1. In a medium mixing bowl, combine the sour cream, cream cheese, vanilla extract or brandy, and sugar and beat with a wooden spoon until light and fluffy.

2. Fold in the coconut, strawberries, and 2 tablespoons of the hazelnuts. Mix well.

3. Spread generously on bread slices and serve open-faced, dusted with the remaining hazelnuts. Or press into a crock, top with the remaining nuts, and serve at room temperature or chilled.

Note: Shredded unsweetened coconut is available in health food stores and gourmet groceries. To toast coconut, place on a baking sheet in a preheated 350°F oven until slightly brown on the edges, 5 to 6 minutes.

Fruit and Spice Mascarpone Spread

Makes about 2 cups

$^1/_4$ **pound dried peaches or apricots, chopped**
$^1/_4$ **pound dried cherries or cranberries, chopped**
$^1/_4$ **pound dried blackberries or raspberries, chopped**
3 tablespoons Grand Marnier, kirsch, or other sweet fruit liqueur of choice, or 2 tablespoons orange juice concentrate
$^1/_4$ **cup lemon juice**
1 teaspoon grated lemon zest
1 tablespoon brown sugar or honey
1 whole cinnamon stick
1 to 2 allspice berries, or 1 whole clove
1$^1/_2$ cups mascarpone cheese, room temperature
$^1/_2$ **cup cream cheese or well-drained ricotta, room temperature**
Pinch of salt
Pinch of freshly ground white pepper
1 green apple, peeled, cored, and grated
$^1/_4$ **cup finely chopped toasted hazelnuts, skins rubbed off (see page xiv)**

1. In a small bowl, combine the dried fruit and the liqueur or orange juice concentrate. Let soak until the fruit is softened, about 30 minutes.

2. Place the fruit mixture in a medium, heavy saucepan and add the lemon juice, lemon zest, sugar or honey, cinnamon stick, and allspice berries or clove. Over medium-high heat, cook, stirring constantly, until the sugar dissolves, about 3 minutes. Reduce the heat to low and let simmer until the mixture begins to thicken, about 30 minutes. Remove from the heat and discard the cinnamon stick and allspice berries or clove. Set aside to cool to room temperature.

3. In a medium mixing bowl, combine the mascarpone, cream cheese or ricotta, and salt and pepper; stir to mix well. Stir in the grated apple, the cooled fruit mixture, and the nuts.

4. Transfer to a serving bowl or terrine. Cover with plastic wrap, refrigerate, and serve chilled.

Serve this with a citrus-scented pound cake cut into wedges and toasted in the broiler until slightly golden. Or serve in individual ramekins with well-toasted English muffins or lemon or orange scones. For a luncheon plate, spread a small amount on toasted bread to accompany slices of wine-poached chicken breast.

Fruit Purée

Makes about 1 $^{1}/_{2}$ cups

Serve this thick all-fruit purée as an alternative to butter or as a fruit spread with tea scones or freshly made buttermilk biscuits. It makes a wonderful accompaniment to a piece of brioche toast with mascarpone or cream cheese in place of the standard preserves and butter.

4 pounds fresh fruit, such as peaches, apricots, plums, ripe fresh figs, strawberries, or other berries or fruit of choice, pitted, peeled, and chopped
1 cup sugar
1 cup water

1. In a large nonreactive saucepan, combine all the ingredients. Bring to a boil and cook until the fruit is very tender throughout.

2. Transfer to the bowl of a food processor fitted with the metal blade and process to a purée. If desired, strain to remove any seeds or pulp that remain.

3. Return the fruit purée to the saucepan and cook, partially covered, over very low heat. Stirring frequently, reduce by about half the original amount or until the purée is thick, about 2 hours.

4. Let cool to room temperature. Transfer the purée to sterilized glass containers and refrigerate covered until ready to use.

Sweet Cheese and Fresh Figs

Makes about $^3/_4$ cup

$^1/_2$ cup mascarpone or cream cheese, regular or low-fat
2 teaspoons brandy or cognac
1 tablespoon sugar
$^1/_4$ cup peeled, well-trimmed, chopped fresh figs

1. In the bowl of a food processor fitted with the metal blade, combine the cheese, brandy or cognac, and sugar. Process to a smooth spread. Fold in the figs.

2. Transfer to a crock or serving dish and serve at room temperature. Or cover with plastic wrap, refrigerate, and serve chilled.

Variation

Sweet Cheese and Fresh Cherries

Substitute cherry liqueur (kirsch) for the brandy or cognac. Increase the sugar by 1 teaspoon and substitute pitted, chopped fresh cherries for the figs.

Serve this dessert or teatime spread on a slice of country-style bread or delicate crustless toast points, on a slice of citrus-scented pound cake, with a homemade shortbread cookie, or on an English muffin.

Chocolate Espresso Spread

Makes about $2/3$ cup

This intense-flavored spread is similar in taste to the popular Italian dessert called tiramisu. Spread it on graham crackers or cookies, or make elegant dessert sandwiches by placing a spoonful of spread between thin slices of cake.

$1/2$ cup mascarpone cheese or low-fat cream cheese, room temperature
1 tablespoon Dutch-process cocoa powder (unsweetened)
1 tablespoon instant espresso powder, dissolved in 1 teaspoon warm water
2 tablespoons confectioners' sugar
1 teaspoon vanilla extract or brandy

1. In a small bowl, whisk the cheese until light.

2. In another small bowl, combine the cocoa powder, espresso, and sugar. Add a small amount of the cheese and stir into a paste. Add a little more of the cheese and mix well. Fold that mixture into the remaining cheese. Stir in the vanilla extract or brandy.

3. Transfer to a small serving bowl and serve immediately.

Toppers

Fresh Herb and Scallion Topper

Makes about 2 1/2 cups

2 cups ricotta, regular or part-skim, well drained
1/4 cup plus 2 tablespoons chopped fresh herbs of choice, such as savory, parsley, basil, and chervil
2 tablespoons extra virgin olive oil
4 scallions, white and most of green parts, finely chopped
Salt
Freshly ground black pepper

1. In a small bowl, place the ricotta and break up any lumps with a fork. Add the herbs, olive oil, scallions, and salt and pepper to taste. Stir and then whip with the fork to mix until thoroughly combined.

2. Transfer to a serving dish and serve immediately. Or cover with plastic wrap, refrigerate, and serve chilled.

Serve this creamy topper on tiny new potatoes, halved and oven roasted, or stuffed into Fresh Cucumber and Zucchini Cups (page 171), raw mushroom caps, or seeded cherry tomatoes. Press into a ramekin and serve chilled or at room temperature with grilled or toasted bread, or crackers.

Greek Garlic Topper (Skordalia)

Makes about 2 1/2 cups

This traditional Greek appetizer pairs well with broccoli and cauliflower florets, vegetable slices such as cucumber, zucchini, and beets, or snow-pea pods and green beans. It's great as a topper for many cooked foods, including grilled or broiled fish or chicken strips.

3 slices white bread, crusts removed, bread torn into small pieces
1 cup blanched almonds, very finely ground
4 to 6 cloves garlic, finely chopped
Pinch of salt
3 tablespoons fresh lemon juice
3/4 cup extra virgin olive oil

1. In the bowl of a food processor fitted with the metal blade, place the bread and pulse several times until small pieces form. Add the ground almonds, garlic, and salt and continue processing to a paste. Pour in the lemon juice and process to mix well.

2. With the motor running, add a few drops of oil at a time. Process until the mixture is thick and creamy. Add only enough oil to achieve a light and fluffy consistency. (You may not need to use all of the oil.)

3. Transfer to a serving bowl and serve immediately.

Cilantro Chutney

Makes about $^1/_2$ cup

1 cup finely chopped cilantro
2 to 3 shallots, finely chopped
Juice of 1$^1/_2$ lemons
$^1/_2$ teaspoon chili powder
1 teaspoon ground cumin
Pinch of salt

1. In a small bowl, combine all the ingredients and stir to mix well.

2. Place in a serving bowl. Serve at room temperature.

Mint and Parsley Chutney

Makes about 1 cup

$^1/_2$ cup chopped fresh mint

$^1/_2$ cup chopped flat-leaf parsley

$^1/_2$ serrano or jalapeño chile, seeded, deveined, and finely chopped (see page xiv)

Juice of 1 lemon or lime

$^1/_2$ to 1 teaspoon mild or hot curry powder (Madras or best quality available)

1. In a small bowl, combine all the ingredients and stir to mix well.

2. Transfer to a serving bowl. Serve at room temperature.

Crunchy Black Bean Topper

Makes about 2 cups

1/2 pound dried black beans, rinsed, or 1 1/2 cups canned, rinsed
  and well drained
4 cups water
2 to 3 tablespoons extra virgin olive oil
2 cloves garlic, finely chopped
4 shallots, thinly sliced
Salt
Freshly ground black pepper
1/2 cup thinly sliced celery
3 to 4 tablespoons chopped flat-leaf parsley or cilantro

1. If using dried beans: In a large, heavy saucepan, combine the beans and water. Bring to a boil, lower the heat, and cook, uncovered, until the beans are just done and still slightly crunchy, about 1 1/4 hours. Check for doneness after 45 minutes. Place in a strainer to drain well and cool. If using canned beans, begin with step 2.

2. In a medium, heavy skillet or sauté pan, heat the olive oil over medium heat. Add the garlic and shallots and cook until translucent, about 3 minutes. Add the beans, stir to mix, and season to taste with salt and pepper.

3. Place the bean mixture in a bowl and let cool to room temperature. Toss in the celery and the parsley or cilantro and transfer to a serving dish. Serve at room temperature.

Serve this fresh and healthy topper with Fresh Cucumber and Zucchini Cups (see page 171) or use Belgian endive leaves as a natural scoop.

Green Lentil and Onion Topper

Makes about 2 cups

This recipe calls for Le Puy lentils, a tiny green variety often used in France. They can be found at most gourmet markets. Brown lentils are a perfect substitute. Serve this topper piled into Fresh Cucumber and Zucchini Cups (see page 171) for a super-hearty appetizer or as a low-fat lunch or vegetable main dish.

$1/2$ pound tiny green Le Puy lentils or brown or red lentils
4 cups water
1 to 2 cloves garlic, finely chopped
1 teaspoon salt, or more to taste
2 tablespoons extra virgin olive oil
1 teaspoon crushed red pepper flakes, or $1/4$ teaspoon cayenne pepper
2 scallions, white and some green parts, chopped
1 red onion, quartered and thinly sliced
3 tablespoons chopped flat-leaf parsley

1. In a medium, heavy saucepan, combine the lentils, water, garlic, and 1 teaspoon salt. Bring to a boil, reduce the heat to low, and cook, uncovered, until the lentils are tender, 20 to 25 minutes. Test for doneness after 15 minutes. Place in a strainer to drain well.

2. In a medium mixing bowl, place the lentils, drizzle with the olive oil, add the crushed red pepper or cayenne, and toss to mix well. Stir in the scallions and red onion and add more salt if needed. Stir in 2 tablespoons of the parsley and marinate at room temperature for 30 minutes.

3. Transfer to a serving bowl and sprinkle with the remaining parsley before serving.

Variation

Sun-Dried Tomato and Lentil Dip

Place the completed mixture in the bowl of a food processor fitted with the metal blade. Add 2 tablespoons chopped sun-dried tomatoes that have been soaked in chicken broth for 30 minutes, excess moisture squeezed out. Process to a smooth purée. Serve as a dip with vegetables or pita chips.

White Bean Mousse

Makes about 3 cups

3 cups canned white canellini or Great Northern beans
1/2 cup extra virgin olive oil
1/4 cup whole milk, warmed
2 teaspoons dried herbs of choice, such as oregano and thyme
2 flat anchovy fillets, drained and chopped (optional)
Juice of 1 lemon, or to taste
Salt
Freshly ground black pepper, plus a few turns of the peppermill

1. In the bowl of a food processor fitted with the metal blade, process the beans to a smooth purée. Transfer to a medium, heavy saucepan and warm the bean purée over low heat, stirring constantly. Remove the pan from the heat.

2. Add the olive oil a few drops at a time at first, then in small amounts, stirring and whipping the beans until a stiff purée forms. Add the milk in small amounts, whipping the purée into a fluffy mousse. (You may not need to use all of the milk.) Stir in the herbs, anchovies if using, and lemon juice. Season to taste with salt and pepper.

3. Transfer to a shallow serving bowl and serve immediately at room temperature. Top with a few turns of the peppermill.

This spread is a lighter, fluffy version of Italian White Bean Pâté (page 10). Serve it piled on toasted rustic bread or crackers. It also makes a good butter substitute with bread at the dinner table.

Sun-Dried Tomato and Olive Tapenade

Makes about 1 cup

Serve this flavorful topper with fresh country-style bread or baguette croûtes.

3 ounces dry-packed sun-dried tomatoes, softened in very hot water, squeezed dry, and coarsely chopped
1 tablespoon small capers, rinsed, drained, and patted dry
5 ounces pitted Niçoise olives
1 clove garlic, finely chopped
1 teaspoon grated lemon zest
1 teaspoon fresh lemon juice
$1/_2$ teaspoon dried herbes de Provence, thyme, or rosemary
3 tablespoons extra virgin olive oil
Salt

1. In the bowl of a food processor fitted with the metal blade, combine all the ingredients except the salt and process to a coarse purée. Season to taste with salt.

2. Transfer to a bowl and serve at room temperature, or store in a tightly covered container in the refrigerator or freezer.

Mixed Olive Tapenade

Makes about 1 1/2 cups

1/2 cup finely chopped pitted Italian olives
1/2 cup finely chopped pitted black olives
1/4 cup finely chopped pitted Niçoise olives
1/2 jalapeño or serrano chile, seeded, deveined, and finely chopped
   (see page xiv), optional
1 tablespoon small capers, rinsed and drained
1/2 cup finely chopped flat-leaf parsley
1 tablespoon finely chopped fresh basil
2 teaspoons honey
2 teaspoons balsamic vinegar
2 tablespoons white wine vinegar
Freshly ground black pepper

1. In a small mixing bowl, combine all the ingredients except the black pepper and stir to combine. Marinate at room temperature for 30 minutes.

2. Drain the liquid from the mixture and season to taste with pepper. Serve at room temperature.

For entertaining, serve this elegant tapenade along with a selection of other toppers, such as creamy pesto or salsa. Or simply use it to top hot potato skins.

Chunky Artichoke and Brie Pâté

Makes about 2 cups

Serve this quick and easy spread with crisp crackers.

1 shallot, finely chopped
1 pound French or domestic Brie cheese, roughly chopped
$^1/_4$ cup finely chopped flat-leaf parsley
$^1/_2$ cup marinated artichoke hearts, well drained and roughly chopped
$^1/_2$ teaspoon grated lemon zest or well-rinsed and drained small capers
2 tablespoons dry sherry, or to taste
Salt
Freshly ground white pepper

1. In the bowl of a food processor fitted with the metal blade, combine the shallot, Brie, parsley, artichoke hearts, lemon zest or capers, and 1 tablespoon of the sherry. Process to a coarse consistency. The artichoke pieces will make the texture slightly chunky.

2. Add the remaining sherry and season to taste with salt and white pepper.

3. Press into a crock or terrine and serve at room temperature.

Variations

Green Bell Pepper and Brie Pâté

Instead of marinated artichoke hearts, use equal amounts of green bell pepper and sautéed red onion.

Salsa and Brie Spread

Instead of marinated artichoke hearts, use an equal amount of a salsa of choice (pages 80–85, 103, 104), drained.

Melted Brie Topper

Makes about 1 1/2 cups

2 tablespoons Roasted Garlic Purée (page 3)
4 to 6 dry-packed sun-dried tomato halves, soaked in warm water for
   10 minutes, drained, dried, and chopped
1 teaspoon dried rosemary, crumbled
One 1-pound wheel French or domestic Brie cheese
1 tablespoon finely chopped flat-leaf parsley, or 2 tablespoons finely
   chopped fresh basil

Top slices of fresh or toasted baguette, apple or pear, or raw vegetables.

1. Preheat the oven to 375°F.

2. In a small bowl, combine the garlic purée, sun-dried tomatoes, and rosemary. Set aside.

3. Carefully remove the rind just from the top of the Brie and discard. Place in an ovenproof baking dish just slightly larger than the wheel. Spread the garlic mixture evenly over the top of the cheese.

4. Bake until the cheese is soft inside, about 10 minutes. Carefully transfer to a shallow bowl or plate and sprinkle with the parsley or basil. Serve immediately.

Creamy Hot Crab and Salsa Topper

Makes about 1 1/2 cups

Serve this ever-popular topper with an assortment of crisp crackers.

1 pound low-fat cream cheese, room temperature
1/2 pound fresh or canned lump crabmeat, well drained (liquid reserved) and picked over for any remaining shell
1 tablespoon liquid from crab or chicken broth
1 cup salsa of choice (pages 80–85), drained

1. In a medium mixing bowl, using a wire whisk or wooden spoon, whip the cream cheese until smooth.

2. Add the remaining ingredients and stir to mix well. Continue whipping to lighten the mixture.

3. Place the mixture in a microwave- and flame-proof dish and cover tightly with plastic wrap. Place in the microwave on high until bubbling and hot throughout, 2 to 3 minutes. Remove the plastic wrap and discard.

4. Preheat the broiler. Broil until the top is golden brown and bubbling, about 1 minute. Serve immediately.

Variations

Instead of crab, use well-drained canned albacore tuna, cooked lobster, or shrimp.

Spicy Yogurt Topper

Makes about 2 cups

1 teaspoon chili powder, or to taste
1 teaspoon ground coriander, or to taste
2 cups plain Yogurt Cheese (page 28), drained at least 4 hours
1¹/₂ teaspoons packed brown sugar or honey
Salt

1. In a small cast-iron skillet or heavy nonstick pan, toast the chili powder and coriander over medium-high heat until fragrant, 30 to 40 seconds. Remove from the pan immediately and place the spices on a plate to cool.

2. Place the yogurt cheese in a mixing bowl and break apart with a fork. Add the brown sugar or honey and salt to taste. Sprinkle in the spices and stir until all the ingredients are well incorporated.

3. Transfer to a crock or terrine and serve at room temperature. Or cover with plastic wrap, refrigerate, and serve chilled.

Serve this creamy, thick topper on potato skins or with Green Lentil and Onion Topper (page 60) alongside a basket of flatbread or flour tortillas. Feel free to reduce the amount of spices for a milder-tasting topper.

Herbed Goat Cheese and Sautéed Red Onion Topper

Makes about 1 cup

Pile a spoonful on top a crisp sesame cracker or mini corn blini. Fill Fresh Cucumber and Zucchini Cups (page 171) for a calorie-wise bite-size appetizer.

3/4 to 1 cup fresh chèvre (see page 23), such as Montrachet, room temperature
2 tablespoons chopped fresh thyme
2 cloves garlic, pressed
Salt
Freshly ground black pepper
2 tablespoons extra virgin olive oil
4 medium red or Spanish onions, thinly sliced
1 tablespoon sugar

1. In a small mixing bowl, combine the chèvre, 1 tablespoon of the thyme, and the garlic. Add salt and pepper to taste and whisk until fluffy and well combined.

2. Lightly coat a wide, shallow bowl with cooking spray or line with plastic wrap. Firmly press the cheese mixture into the bowl. Refrigerate for 30 minutes.

3. Meanwhile, in a medium, heavy skillet, heat the oil over medium-high heat. Add the onions and cook until lightly browned. Sprinkle with sugar, season with salt and pepper, and stir to mix well. Continue cooking over low heat until the onions deepen in color and caramelize. Stir in the remaining 1 tablespoon of thyme and keep warm.

4. Unmold the cheese on a serving platter. Let come to room temperature. Top the cheese mold with the onions, covering completely. Serve immediately.

Aged Goat Cheese in Herbs and Olive Oil

Makes about $^1/_2$ cup

8 ounces aged chèvre (see page 23), sliced

1 to 2 tablespoons olive oil, flavored (garlic, herb, or pink peppercorn) if desired

1 to 2 tablespoons chopped mixed fresh herbs, such as chervil, thyme, basil, flat-leaf parsley, dill, and oregano

1. Place the cheese slices in a pottery or glass serving dish. Drizzle with the olive oil and sprinkle with fresh herbs.

2. Cover with plastic wrap and refrigerate for 2 to 4 hours or longer to marinate. Serve at room temperature.

This is an instant topper that can be prepared in advance and kept in the refrigerator.

Goat Cheese and Caviar Topper

Makes about 1 cup

Before topping with this elegant combination of ingredients, remove the crusts from slices of fresh white bread, cut into quarters, and toast but do not brown.

8 ounces unaged chèvre (see page 23)
2 tablespoons sour cream
1 ounce golden or dark caviar (best quality available)

1. Place the cheese in a bowl, add the sour cream, and stir until smooth and fluffy.

2. Spoon the chèvre mixture into a shallow serving bowl and smooth the top. Chill for 30 minutes. Carefully spread the caviar over the top and cover completely. Serve immediately.

Creamy Caramelized Shallot and Onion Topper

Makes about 2 cups

1 tablespoon unsalted butter
1 large yellow onion, sliced into thin rounds
6 to 8 large shallots, very thinly sliced
1 to 2 tablespoons Roasted Garlic Purée (page 3), or to taste
1 cup low-fat cream cheese, room temperature
2 scallions, white and some green parts, chopped
2 tablespoons finely chopped flat-leaf parsley
1 teaspoon dried herbes de Provence or a combination of dried thyme, basil, marjoram, and parsley
Salt
Freshly ground black pepper

1. In a medium, heavy skillet or sauté pan, melt the butter over medium heat. Add the onion and shallots and cook in a single layer for about 15 minutes. Press down on the layer with a spatula once or twice during cooking but do not stir. Turn over the onion like a pancake and cook the other side until caramelized, about 10 minutes more. Transfer to a plate and set aside to cool to room temperature.

2. In the bowl of a food processor fitted with the metal blade, combine the garlic purée and the caramelized onion. Process to a purée. Add the cream cheese, scallions, parsley, and dried herbs. Pulse several times until well blended and smooth. Season to taste with salt and pepper.

3. Transfer to a serving bowl and serve immediately. Or transfer to a tightly covered container and refrigerate until ready to use. Serve at room temperature.

Serve a dollop of this on top of mashed white or sweet potatoes instead of sour cream or butter. It also can be tossed with pasta or rice.

Layered Ricotta Terrine

Makes about 5 cups

Spoon a dollop on top of Rustic Croûtes (page 152), Polenta Crisps (page 169), or a variety of grilled light and dark bread slices. Or serve with a crudité assortment.

4 cups part-skim ricotta, well drained (for at least 1 hour)
1 cup low-fat cream cheese
Pinch of cayenne pepper
$1/2$ teaspoon salt
1 teaspoon freshly ground white pepper
$1/4$ cup chopped scallion, white and green parts chopped separately
$1/4$ cup finely chopped mixed fresh herbs, such as chervil, tarragon, basil, parsley, marjoram, and chives
$1/4$ cup toasted sesame seeds (see page xiv)
$1/4$ cup finely chopped red bell pepper
$1/4$ cup chopped toasted nuts (see page xiv), such as walnuts, hazelnuts, or pistachios

1. In a medium mixing bowl, combine the ricotta and cream cheese with the cayenne, salt, white pepper, and white part of the scallion.

2. In a serving terrine large enough to hold all the ingredients, cover the bottom with one-quarter of the cheese mixture and top with the herbs. Gently spread on another quarter of the cheese and then sprinkle on the sesame seeds. Spread on another quarter of the cheese and top with the red bell pepper. Top with the remaining cheese and sprinkle with the nuts and green part of the scallion.

3. Cover the terrine with plastic wrap and refrigerate. Serve well chilled.

Getting the Best of Ricotta

The ricotta we buy in the supermarket (which is actually a by-product of cheese making) is usually much too moist to use in spreads, toppers, and dips. To drain off all visible liquid, line a colander with 3 to 4 pieces of cheesecloth. Spoon in the ricotta and allow to drain for at least 1 hour. The longer it drains, the denser and thicker it becomes. In certain recipes a longer draining time is required. Follow recipe directions when this occurs.

Fresh Herb and
Avocado Fromage Topper

Makes about 2¹/₂ cups

1 ripe Haas avocado, halved, pitted, and flesh scooped out
2 cups regular or part-skim ricotta, drained for 2 to 4 hours
4 to 6 tablespoons mixed chopped fresh seasonal herbs, such as savory,
    parsley, basil, and chervil
3 to 4 scallions, white and light green parts, finely chopped
2 tablespoons extra virgin olive oil
Salt
Freshly ground black or white pepper

1. In a medium mixing bowl, mash the avocado, leaving some texture. Add the ricotta and mash with a fork to break up any lumps. Stir in the herbs and scallions.

2. Add the olive oil a little at a time and whip to incorporate before adding more. Season to taste with salt and pepper.

3. Transfer to a serving dish and serve immediately. Or cover with plastic wrap, refrigerate, and serve chilled. Make sure the plastic wrap is touching the top of the mixture to prevent air from turning it dark.

Note: Haas avocados have a dark, bumpy peel and are more suitable in flavor for avocado-based spreads, toppers, and dips.

Serve this versatile and surprisingly light avocado-cheese combination as a topper for Bruschetta (page 151) or Crostini (page 154). Try it paired with crackers such as homemade Polenta Crisps (page 169) for a crispy alternative to fried corn tortilla chips. Or use it on Roasted Curried Potato Wedges (page 160), in Fresh Cucumber and Zucchini Cups (page 171), or stuffed into scooped-out cherry tomatoes or raw mushroom caps.

Warm Brandy and Mushroom Pâté

Makes about 2 cups

Serve this hearty vegetarian topper on Rustic Croûtes (pages 152–153) or crackers, on pasta and baked potatoes, or as a substitute for meat, poultry, or cheese toppers.

¹/₄ cup (¹/₂ stick) unsalted butter
6 cups roughly chopped mixed fresh wild and cultivated mushrooms, such as oyster, shiitake, cremini, Portobello, and white button mushrooms
¹/₄ cup best-quality brandy or cognac
¹/₄ cup plus 2 tablespoons sour cream, regular or low-fat, or crème fraîche (see Note, page 44)
2 tablespoons chopped fresh tarragon
3 tablespoons chopped flat-leaf parsley
Salt
Freshly ground black pepper

1. In a medium skillet or sauté pan, melt the butter over medium heat. Add the mushrooms and sauté until they release their liquid and most of it evaporates, about 5 minutes.

2. Lower the heat and add the brandy or cognac and sour cream or crème fraîche. Stir to mix and cook until the mixture thickens. Stir in the tarragon and 1 tablespoon of the parsley. Season to taste with salt and pepper.

3. Press into a terrine or serve in individual ramekins. Sprinkle with the remaining parsley. Serve warm.

Sautéed Portobello Mushroom Topper

Makes about 1 1/2 cups

3 tablespoons unsalted butter
1 pound fresh Portobello or white button mushrooms, washed, trimmed, dried, and roughly chopped
2 cloves garlic, chopped
1/2 cup chopped scallions, white and some green parts
2 tablespoons fresh lemon juice
1 tablespoon balsamic vinegar
1 tablespoon extra virgin olive oil
1/2 cup chopped mixed fresh herbs, such as thyme, tarragon, and parsley
Salt
Freshly ground black pepper
Pinch of ground nutmeg

1. In a medium, heavy skillet, melt 2 tablespoons of the butter over medium-high heat. Add the mushrooms and cook until they release their liquid and it evaporates. Transfer to the bowl of a food processor fitted with the metal blade. Set aside.

2. In the same skillet, melt the remaining butter over medium heat. Add the garlic and scallions and cook until tender but not browned.

3. Add the scallions to the mushrooms. Add the lemon juice, vinegar, olive oil, and fresh herbs and process to a slightly coarse consistency. Season to taste with salt and pepper and add the nutmeg. Process just to mix.

4. Transfer to a serving bowl and serve warm or at room temperature.

Variation

Creamy Portobello Spread

Stir in 2 to 3 tablespoons crème fraîche (see Note, page 44) or sour cream along with the salt and pepper. Process to a smooth consistency. Press into a crock or terrine and serve warm.

Eggplant Caviar

Makes about 1 1/2 cups

Serve this with fresh vegetables, Rustic Croûtes (pages 152–153), or fresh French baguette slices.

1 large or 2 medium eggplants
1 tablespoon extra virgin olive oil
1 medium red bell pepper, diced
1 small onion, finely chopped
2 cloves garlic, finely chopped
1 large ripe tomato (vine-ripened if available), peeled, seeded, and diced
1 tablespoon fresh lemon juice, or to taste
3 tablespoons finely chopped scallion, light and dark green parts, or chives
1 tablespoon finely chopped fresh basil
Salt
Freshly ground black pepper

1. Preheat the oven to 350°F.

2. Cut the eggplant in half lengthwise, place on a baking sheet cut side down, and bake for 1 hour. Scoop out the flesh and place in the bowl of a food processor fitted with the metal blade. Process to a purée and set aside.

3. In a small skillet or sauté pan, heat 2 teaspoons of the olive oil over medium heat. Add the red bell pepper, onion, and garlic and cook, stirring occasionally, until the vegetables are tender but not browned, about 5 minutes. Transfer to a large mixing bowl and let cool to room temperature.

4. Add the eggplant purée to the mixing bowl, along with the tomato, lemon juice, scallion or chives, basil, and remaining olive oil. Stir to mix well and season to taste with salt and pepper.

5. Transfer to a serving bowl. Serve at room temperature.

Cucumber and Yogurt Topper
(Tzatziki)

Makes about 1¹/₂ cups

1 cup plain yogurt, regular or low-fat, or, for thicker topper,
   Yogurt Cheese (page 28)
1 hothouse cucumber, peeled, seeded, grated, and moisture squeezed out
   (about ³/₄ cup cucumber)
3 tablespoons chopped fresh mint
2 cloves garlic, pressed
Salt
Freshly ground black pepper

1. In a small mixing bowl, combine the yogurt or yogurt cheese, cucumber, mint, and garlic. Stir to mix well. Season to taste with salt and pepper.

2. Transfer to a serving bowl and serve immediately. Or cover with plastic wrap, refrigerate, and serve chilled.

Serve as an hors d'oeuvre as they do in Greece, with an assortment of olives, fresh cucumber slices, fresh crusty country bread, and a tiny glass of ouzo.

Mediterranean Vegetable Topper
(Caponata Antipasto)

Makes about 3 cups

Serve this as part of an antipasto or appetizer assortment. Caponata is great piled on crispy garlic croûtes or accompanied by warmed fresh, crusty, country-style garlic bread.

1 large or 2 medium eggplants
Coarse salt
$1/4$ cup extra virgin olive oil
1 medium red onion, finely chopped
1 medium yellow onion, finely chopped
2 ribs celery, leaves removed, finely chopped
1 medium red bell pepper, trimmed and cut into 1-inch pieces
1 medium yellow bell pepper, trimmed and cut into 1-inch pieces
1 medium green bell pepper, trimmed and cut into 1-inch pieces
2 medium zucchini, finely chopped
$1/2$ cup tomato purée
$1/2$ cup dry red wine, such as pinot noir
1 tablespoon balsamic vinegar
1 tablespoon honey
1 tablespoon pine nuts
10 black olives, pitted and chopped
10 green olives, pitted and chopped
Salt
Freshly ground black pepper

1. Peel the eggplant and cut into 1-inch cubes. Sprinkle with coarse salt, set in a colander, and let drain in a colander for $1/2$ hour. Rinse well and pat dry with paper towels.

2. In a large, heavy skillet or sauté pan, heat 2 tablespoons of the olive oil over medium-high heat. Add the eggplant and cook until lightly browned and tender. Turn onto several layers of paper towels to absorb any excess oil.

3. In another heavy skillet or sauté pan, heat the remaining 2 tablespoons of olive oil over medium heat. Add the onions and celery and cook until tender.

4. Add the peppers and zucchini and cook until the onions are golden and the peppers and zucchini are tender. Add the tomato purée and continue cooking over medium-low heat until the liquid has turned syrupy, about 10 minutes.

5. Add the wine, vinegar, honey, pine nuts, olives, and eggplant. Stir and continue cooking until no visible moisture is remaining in the skillet, about 2 minutes more. Season to taste with salt and pepper. Let cool to room temperature before serving.

Salsas

Salsas make good "sideline" flavorings for many popular finger foods, such as tempura vegetables, Roasted Curried Potato Wedges (page 160), or skewered and grilled fish, chicken, or meat.

Mix with Yogurt Cheese (page 28) or butter (page 7).

Mix with ricotta cheese and sour cream.

Spicy Fresh Tomato Salsa

Makes about 3 cups

4 to 6 large ripe tomatoes, peeled, seeded, and roughly chopped (about 3 cups)
2 serrano or jalapeño chilies, seeded and deveined (see page xiv), chopped,
    or more or less to taste
2 small red onions, quartered
2 cloves garlic, chopped
$^1/_4$ cup plus 1 tablespoon finely chopped cilantro
2 tablespoons red wine vinegar or lemon juice
1 teaspoon salt

1. In the bowl of a food processor fitted with the metal blade, place the tomatoes and pulse several times to chop coarsely. Transfer the tomatoes to a medium glass or pottery serving bowl and set aside.

2. Place the chilies, onions, and garlic in the food processor and process until finely chopped. Add to the tomatoes.

3. Stir in the cilantro, vinegar or lemon juice, and salt. Cover with plastic wrap, refrigerate, and serve chilled.

Red Onion, Tomato, and Avocado Salsa

Makes about 2 $^1/_2$ cups

2 cups seeded and diced ripe tomatoes
1 medium red onion, quartered and thinly sliced or chopped
$^1/_2$ jalapeño chile, seeded and very finely chopped (see page xiv),
   or $^1/_4$ teaspoon red pepper flakes, ground or crushed
1 ripe Haas avocado, halved, pitted, peeled,
   and diced small
1 tablespoon fresh lemon or lime juice
Salt

1. In a medium bowl, combine all the ingredients and stir. Season to taste with salt and mix well.

2. Transfer to a glass or pottery serving dish. Serve at room temperature, or cover with plastic wrap, refrigerate, and serve chilled.

Roasted Tomato Salsa

Makes about 3 cups

6 to 8 ripe tomatoes (about 2 pounds)
1 large onion, unpeeled
2 to 3 cloves garlic, unpeeled
1 small serrano or jalapeño chile, seeded and halved (see page xiv)
1 teaspoon salt, plus more to taste
1 tablespoon canola oil or extra virgin olive oil
1/2 teaspoon finely chopped cilantro
1 tablespoon fresh lemon juice
Pinch of sugar

1. Preheat the oven to 400°F.

2. Place the tomatoes and onion in a roasting pan and roast until the tomato skins are blackened, about 1 hour. Let cool and peel, making sure to remove all the charred peel. Roughly chop the tomatoes and onion.

3. In a cast-iron skillet, cook the garlic cloves and chile over medium heat, turning frequently, until soft throughout. Let cool.

4. Peel the garlic and place with the chile in the bowl of a food processor fitted with the metal blade. Process until finely chopped. Add the tomatoes, onion, 1 teaspoon salt, oil, cilantro, and lemon juice and pulse to a slightly textured purée. Add the sugar and more salt to taste.

5. Transfer to a serving bowl and serve at room temperature.

Cucumber Papaya Salsa

1 ripe papaya, peeled, seeded, and diced
2 hothouse or regular cucumbers, peeled, seeded, diced, and drained in
   a strainer for 20 minutes
$1/2$ to 1 teaspoon crushed red pepper flakes
2 to 3 scallions, white and most of green parts, chopped
2 tablespoons finely chopped fresh mint
2 tablespoons fresh lemon or lime juice
1 tablespoon tequila, white rum, or citrus vodka
2 tablespoons sugar, or 1 tablespoon honey
Pinch of salt

1. In a medium pottery or glass mixing bowl, combine all the ingredients.

2. Transfer to a serving dish. Serve at room temperature, or cover with plastic wrap, refrigerate, and serve chilled.

Variation

Substitute $1^1/_2$ cups diced other fruits, such as melon, pineapple, peaches, apples, or pears for the papaya. Add $1/_4$ cup orange juice or more for fruits that are not naturally juicy.

For Spread recipes using this salsa, see page 9.

Tomato Poblano Salsa

Makes about 1 1/2 cups

2 poblano chilies, roasted, seeded, and peeled (see page xiv)
1 small jalapeño chile, stemmed, deveined, seeded,
    and finely chopped (see page xiv)
1 to 2 cloves garlic, finely chopped
1/4 cup chopped cilantro
1/2 small red onion, roughly chopped
3 ripe tomatoes, peeled, seeded, and roughly chopped
1 teaspoon salt
Juice of 1 lemon or lime
2 tablespoons olive oil

1. In the bowl of a food processor fitted with the metal blade, combine the poblanos, jalapeño, garlic, cilantro, and onion. Pulse a few times until minced.

2. Add the tomatoes and pulse several times until roughly chopped. Do not overprocess.

3. Transfer to a glass or pottery serving bowl. Stir in the salt, lemon or lime juice, and olive oil. Serve at room temperature.

Green Tomatillo Salsa

Makes about 1 cup

¹/₂ **pound fresh tomatillos (see Note), papery husks removed, cored,
  and quartered**
1 clove garlic, chopped
**1 to 2 serrano chilies, stemmed, deveined, seeded,
  and finely chopped (see page xiv)**
Pinch of salt
¹/₃ **cup water**
¹/₄ **medium white onion, chopped**
2 tablespoons roughly chopped cilantro

1. Place the tomatillos in the bowl of a food processor fitted with the metal blade and process until finely chopped. Transfer to a bowl and set aside.

2. Place the garlic, chilies, and salt in the food processor and process until finely chopped. Add the water and onion and process until the onion is chopped. Stir into the tomatillo mixture. Add the cilantro. Stir to mix well.

3. Transfer to a serving dish. Serve at room temperature.

Note: The tomatillo, belonging to the tomato family, looks like a small green tomato with a papery husk. Its unique flavor has hints of lemon, apple, and herbs.

Tomato Chutney (Ketchup)

Makes about 3 cups

Serve this with French fries, Roasted Curried Potato Wedges (page 160), or anything ketchup would enhance. Chilled, it is perfect with crisp fresh crudités.

4 cups drained canned plum tomatoes, coarsely chopped
$1/2$ cup tomato paste
1 teaspoon garlic, finely chopped
1 teaspoon fresh ginger, finely chopped
$1/2$ cup chopped onion
$1/2$ cup dark or golden raisins
$1/4$ cup sugar
2 tablespoons balsamic vinegar
$1/2$ cup red wine vinegar
$1/2$ teaspoon salt, plus more to taste
Pinch of cayenne pepper

1. In an enamel or stainless steel saucepan, combine all the ingredients except the cayenne. Bring to a boil, lower the heat, and simmer, uncovered, stirring frequently, until the mixture is very thick, 45 to 50 minutes. Add more salt to taste and the cayenne. Let cool to room temperature.

2. In the bowl of a food processor fitted with the metal blade, process the mixture to a smooth purée. Transfer to a serving bowl and serve immediately, or place in a glass jar with a tight-fitting lid and refrigerate until ready to use.

Roasted Tomato, Garlic, and Shallot Relish

Makes about 3 cups

6 to 8 ripe tomatoes (about 2 pounds)
2 large shallots, unpeeled
2 cloves garlic, unpeeled
1 small serrano or jalapeño chile, halved and seeded (see page xiv)
1 teaspoon salt, plus more to taste
3 tablespoons extra virgin olive oil or canola oil
$1/2$ teaspoon finely chopped fresh rosemary
Juice of 1 lemon
1 teaspoon sugar, or to taste

1. Preheat the oven to 400°F.

2. Place the tomatoes, shallots, garlic, and chile in a roasting pan. Sprinkle with 1 teaspoon of the salt. Roast until the tomatoes are blackened, 45 to 50 minutes. Let cool.

3. When cool enough to handle, peel the roasted vegetables. Squeeze the pulp from the garlic cloves into a medium mixing bowl. Scoop out the seeds and visible juice from the tomato and drain in a strainer for a few minutes, then coarsely chop and add to the bowl. Finely chop the shallots and chile and add to the bowl. Pick out and discard any remaining charred bits of peel.

4. Add the oil, rosemary, lemon juice, and sugar. Stir to mix well. Add more salt to taste.

5. Transfer to a serving dish. Serve at room temperature.

Curried Turkey, Tofu, and Golden Raisin Topper

Makes about 1 1/2 cups

Whether topping a slice of toasted dark bread or piped onto crackers to make elegant canapés, this combination of flavors is destined to be a classic.

3 tablespoons unsalted butter
1/2 medium onion, finely chopped
2 tablespoons mild curry powder
3/4 cup dry white wine
1/3 cup chopped golden raisins
Pinch of sugar
1/2 cup firm tofu, drained and blended until smooth
1/4 cup sour cream, regular or low-fat, or crème fraîche (see Note, page 44)
1/2 pound smoked turkey, roughly chopped
1/2 pound roasted turkey breast, roughly chopped
1/4 cup finely chopped scallions, green part only
3 tablespoons chopped blanched almonds

1. In a medium skillet or sauté pan, melt the butter over low heat. Add the onion and cook until translucent. Add the curry powder, wine, and raisins and continue cooking until the liquid has evaporated, about 20 minutes. Transfer to a bowl and set aside to cool.

2. In a medium mixing bowl, combine the sugar, tofu, and sour cream or crème fraîche and stir to mix. Set aside.

3. Add the smoked and fresh turkey to the cooled onion mixture. Add the tofu mixture and mash the turkey into the other ingredients until moistened, leaving some small chunks. Stir in the scallions and 2 tablespoons of the almonds.

4. Press into a terrine or crock. Sprinkle with the remaining nuts and serve at room temperature, or cover with plastic wrap, refrigerate, and serve chilled.

Coarse Country Pâté

Makes about 2 cups

2 tablespoons extra virgin olive oil
$^1/_2$ pound calves' liver, trimmed and sliced into thin strips
2 strips lean bacon, chopped
$^1/_4$ cup dry red wine
1 plum tomato, peeled, seeded, and chopped
4 to 6 large mushrooms, trimmed and coarsely chopped
$^1/_4$ teaspoon ground allspice or nutmeg
2 tablespoons unsalted butter, room temperature
Salt
Freshly ground black pepper

Serve as a topper on toast or crackers, or with a dollop of Roasted Garlic Purée (page 3) on top to create an even more complex and delicious flavor combination.

1. In a medium, heavy skillet or sauté pan, heat the olive oil over high heat. Add the liver strips and bacon and cook, stirring constantly, just until the liver begins to change color. Add the wine, tomato, mushrooms, and allspice or nutmeg. Continue cooking over medium heat until the liquid evaporates and the liver is browned, about 5 minutes.

2. Transfer the liver mixture to the bowl of a food processor fitted with the metal blade. Pulse until the consistency of the mixture is partly smooth and partly chunky. Do not overprocess.

3. Add the butter and pulse several times to mix well. Season to taste with salt and pepper. Transfer to a crock or terrine and serve warm.

Sausage and Sweet Onion Pâté

Makes about 3 cups

Serve this on top of crackers, melba toast, or toasted baguette slices. Consider trying any of the new low-fat sausages on the market, such as chicken or turkey and veal blends, instead of standard Italian sausage.

1 tablespoon unsalted butter
1 tablespoon olive oil
2 sweet onions (Maui, Vidalia, or Walla Walla), finely chopped
3 cloves garlic, finely chopped
1 teaspoon full-flavored dried herbs, such as oregano, tarragon, or rosemary, or to taste
$1/_2$ cup heavy cream, heated
$1^1/_2$ pounds veal, pork, chicken, turkey, or Italian hot or sweet sausage, casings removed
$1/_2$ cup finely chopped flat-leaf parsley
2 large eggs
$1/_4$ cup brandy or cognac
$1/_2$ teaspoon ground cinnamon
$1/_2$ teaspoon ground nutmeg
Salt
Freshly ground black pepper
$1/_2$ cup coarsely chopped toasted walnuts, pistachios, or almonds (see page xiv)

1. Preheat the oven to 350°F.

2. In a large, heavy skillet, melt the butter and olive oil together over medium-high heat. Lower the heat, add the onions and garlic, and cook, stirring constantly, until golden but not brown.

3. In the bowl of a food processor fitted with the metal blade, combine the onion mixture, dried herbs, cream, sausage, parsley, eggs, brandy or cognac, cinnamon, and nutmeg and process to a coarse consistency.

4. Before adding salt and pepper, cook a tablespoon of the mixture in a small skillet over high heat and taste. Add salt and pepper accordingly. Stir in the nuts.

5. Transfer the mixture to an ovenproof $1^1/_2$-quart terrine lined with heavy aluminum foil. Very tightly cover with a double layer of aluminum foil by tucking in the edges around the terrine. Place the terrine in a fairly deep pan, and fill the pan with hot water halfway up the sides of the terrine. Bake until a knife inserted into the center comes out clean and the juices run clear, about 1 hour, less for poultry-base sausages.

6. Pour off any visible juices. Let sit, undisturbed, for 30 minutes. Remove the pâté from the terrine, discard the foil, and place on a serving platter. Let cool to room temperature before serving.

These Days, "Sausage" Is a Whole Different Animal

If your supermarket or butcher is without great sausages, call 1-800-Haut-Dog, and the Jody Maroni Sausage Kingdom will send sausages via next-day delivery. Flavors include Chicken Italian, Chicken/Turkey Chorizo, and dozens more.

Prosciutto and Arugula Topper
(Crostini or Bruschetta)

Makes 1³/₄ cups (12 crostini or 6 bruschetta servings)

This classic Italian flavor combination is served as tiny finger sandwiches called crostini or as bruschetta on larger slices of grilled or broiled olive oil—scented bread. A tray of these makes great hearty starters or hors d'oeuvres at cocktail time.

12 thick baguette slices or 6 thick slices crusty country-style bread
5 tablespoons extra virgin olive oil
1 tablespoon red wine vinegar
1/2 teaspoon freshly ground black pepper
2 ounces arugula leaves, stemmed and chopped (about 1/2 cup)
1 ripe tomato, peeled, seeded, and diced
6 large slices prosciutto, chopped
1 ounce fresh Parmesan cheese, shaved, plus 12 small or 6 large shaved pieces for garnish

1. Lightly brush the bread slices with 2 tablespoons of the olive oil. Toast both sides until golden under the broiler or on a grill.

2. In a jar with a tight-fitting lid, combine the remaining 3 tablespoons olive oil, the vinegar, and pepper. Shake to combine well.

3. In a small mixing bowl, combine the arugula, tomato, and prosciutto. Drizzle with dressing to taste and toss to combine well. Crumble and add the 1 ounce shaved Parmesan and toss lightly. Top the grilled bread slices with equal amounts of the arugula and prosciutto mixture. Place the remaining shaved pieces of Parmesan on top of each crostini or bruschetta. Serve immediately.

Warm Lemon Chicken Topper

Makes about 2$\frac{1}{2}$ cups

3 tablespoons unsalted butter
1 cup mixed fresh wild or cultivated mushrooms, finely chopped
Pinch of salt
Pinch of ground nutmeg
2 cups finely chopped cooked chicken breast (preferably poached)
1 tablespoon all-purpose flour
$\frac{1}{2}$ cup chicken broth, heated
3 tablespoons fresh lemon juice
1 large egg yolk beaten with 1 tablespoon water
Freshly ground black pepper

Serve this as a topper on warm Scallion Pancakes (page 170), crisp toast pieces, or sesame wafers.

1. In a medium, heavy skillet, melt 1$\frac{1}{2}$ tablespoons of the butter over medium heat. Add the mushrooms, salt, and nutmeg and cook for 1 minute, stirring constantly. Lower the heat and continue cooking the mushrooms until soft and their liquid has almost evaporated, 3 to 5 minutes.

2. Add the chicken pieces and cook for 1 minute more. Transfer the mixture to the bowl of a food processor fitted with the metal blade. Process to a coarse pâté. Set aside.

3. In the same skillet, melt the remaining butter over medium heat. Lower the heat, stir in the flour, and cook, stirring constantly, for 1 minute. Add the hot broth and lemon juice in a thin but steady stream and continue stirring until the mixture thickens and is smooth. Remove from the heat.

4. Place the egg yolk in a medium bowl. Add the sauce a few spoonfuls at a time, incorporating the ingredients between each addition. Return the mixture to the skillet, stir to mix well, and cook over very low heat for 1 minute, stirring constantly. Stir in the chicken and mushroom mixture. Add pepper and more salt to taste. Press in a pâté crock or serving dish and serve warm.

Hot Crab Topper

Makes about 2 cups

This easy-to-make topper is usually gone in minutes, so you may want to make two. Serve it with an array of crackers, or spoon it into baked frozen mini pastry shells.

1 cup sour cream, regular or low-fat
2 tablespoons fresh lemon juice
1 tablespoon grated onion
1 teaspoon Worcestershire sauce
3/4 teaspoon dry mustard
1/4 teaspoon garlic powder
Pinch of salt
Pinch of cayenne pepper
1 cup cream cheese, regular or low-fat, at room temperature
1/4 cup grated sharp cheddar cheese
1 pound fresh lump crabmeat, picked clean of any shell pieces, broken apart with a fork and drained
Vegetable oil cooking spray
Sweet or hot paprika for garnish

1. Preheat the oven to 350°F.

2. In a medium mixing bowl, combine the sour cream, lemon juice, onion, Worcestershire sauce, mustard, garlic powder, salt, cayenne, and cream cheese. Whisk until well combined and fluffy. Stir in the cheddar cheese and crabmeat.

3. Coat the inside of a 1 1/2-quart casserole or soufflé dish with cooking spray. Spoon in the crabmeat mixture, lightly sprinkle the top with paprika, and bake until the top bubbles, 30 to 35 minutes. Serve hot.

Fresh Shellfish Topper

Makes 2 cups

3 tablespoons extra virgin olive oil
4 to 6 large fresh sea scallops
6 fresh mussels, removed from shell
6 fresh clams, removed from shell
6 jumbo raw shrimp, peeled and deveined
1 clove garlic, finely chopped
$1/4$ teaspoon crushed red pepper flakes, or more to taste
$1/4$ cup dry white wine
2 ripe tomatoes, peeled, seeded, and chopped
Salt
Freshly ground black pepper
2 tablespoons chopped flat-leaf parsley

1. In a large, heavy sauté pan, heat the olive oil over medium heat. Add the scallops, mussels, clams, shrimp, garlic, and red pepper flakes and cook, stirring constantly, for 2 minutes.

2. Add the wine and tomatoes and cook, stirring occasionally, until the liquid has evaporated, about 3 minutes. Remove the pan from the heat.

3. With a slotted spoon, remove the shellfish from the pan and transfer to a cutting board. Chop until finely diced. Place the tomato mixture in a serving bowl and add the chopped shellfish. Add salt and pepper to taste and stir in the parsley. Cover with plastic wrap, refrigerate, and serve chilled.

Serve this light and fresh-tasting topper in Fresh Cucumber and Zucchini Cups (page 171) or endive spears, rolled up in lettuce leaves, or on roasted beet and blanched carrot rounds. For party canapés, top toast rounds, or spoon into baked frozen mini pastry shells.

Variation

Creamy Shellfish Topper

Fold in $1/4$ to $1/3$ cup sour cream or crème fraîche (see Note, page 44) just before serving.

Fish Mousse

Makes about 2 cups

Poached Salmon and Mustard; Smoked Trout and Horseradish; Fresh Tuna and Wasabi; Sardine and Caper; Smoked Mackerel, Lemon Zest, and Cayenne. Which one will you choose to make? Each varying in taste, they offer a chance to try a new, possibly unique fish, herb, and spice combination. This basic Fish Mousse recipe applies to all of the Variations.

Fish of choice (see Variations)
Flavoring of choice (see Variations)
1 shallot, finely chopped, or 2 scallions, white part only, finely chopped
$^1/_4$ cup plus 1 tablespoon cold water, fish stock, or dry white wine
1 tablespoon unflavored gelatin
1 cup heavy cream, whipped
Salt
Freshly ground white pepper
$^1/_4$ cup finely chopped fresh herb (see Variations)

1. In the bowl of a food processor fitted with the metal blade, process the fish to a coarse consistency. Add the flavoring and the shallot or scallions and pulse just to mix. Set aside.

2. Place the water, broth, or wine in a small saucepan. Sprinkle the gelatin over the liquid and let sit for 1 minute. Cook over very low heat until the gelatin dissolves, about 1 minute.

3. Pour the gelatin into the fish purée, add the whipped cream, and pulse a few times just to blend. Season to taste with salt and pepper. Stir in all but 1 teaspoon of the herb.

4. Spoon the mousse into a terrine and sprinkle with the remaining herb. Cover with plastic wrap and refrigerate until set and well chilled, 1 hour or more. Serve chilled.

Variations

Poached Salmon and Mustard

Fish: $^1/_2$ pound poached fresh salmon
Flavoring: $^1/_4$ to $^1/_2$ teaspoon dry mustard, or 1 tablespoon prepared Dijon-style mustard
Herb: Finely chopped dill

Smoked Trout and Horseradish

Fish: $1/2$ pound smoked trout, well trimmed of skin and bones
Flavoring: 1 teaspoon rinsed and drained prepared horseradish
Herb: Finely chopped parsley

Fresh Tuna and Wasabi

Fish: $3/4$ pound chopped fresh sashimi quality raw tuna
Flavoring: $1/2$ to 1 teaspoon dry wasabi (see Note)
Herb: Finely chopped fresh chives

Note: Wasabi, a Japanese version of horseradish, can be found in Asian food markets or the Asian section of the supermarket.

Sardine and Caper

Fish: $1/3$ to $1/2$ pound freshly cooked or canned sardines, well trimmed
Flavoring: 1 teaspoon small capers (or more to taste), rinsed and drained
Herb: Finely chopped flat-leaf parsley

Smoked Mackerel, Lemon Zest, and Cayenne

Fish: 6 to 8 ounces canned mackerel (or other canned fish such as salmon or dark meat tuna), well drained and picked clean of any visible bones and skin
Flavoring: 1 teaspoon lemon zest and $1/8$ teaspoon cayenne pepper
Herb: Finely chopped flat-leaf parsley or dill

What's more, each and every delicious fish mousse is perfectly suited for a main course at lunch or as the appetizer at dinner, even on the hors d'oeuvre tray when entertaining. Serve them with bagel chips, green apple slices, melba toast, croûtes, or fresh vegetables.

Tuna Tartar Topper

Makes about 2 cups

Serve this with raw vegetable rounds, water crackers, Plain or Spicy Potato Chips (page 166), or home-made unsalted Tortilla Corn Chips (page 165).

1/2 **pound very fresh raw tuna, coarsely chopped**
2 tablespoons extra virgin olive oil
1 1/2 **tablespoons fresh lemon juice**
2 tablespoons chopped fresh chives
Salt
Freshly ground black pepper
1 ounce golden or red caviar (best quality available)

1. In a small mixing bowl, combine the tuna, olive oil, lemon juice, 1 tablespoon of the chives, and salt and pepper to taste. Stir gently to mix well. Cover with plastic wrap and refrigerate to marinate for 1 hour or more.

2. Transfer to a serving dish, top with the golden caviar, and sprinkle with the remaining chives. Serve immediately.

Potted Shrimp

Makes about 2¹/₂ cups

1¹/₂ cups fish or chicken broth
1 tablespoon unflavored gelatin
2 tablespoons fresh lemon juice
1 teaspoon grated lemon zest
¹/₄ teaspoon cayenne pepper
1¹/₄ pounds cooked shrimp, chopped
2 tablespoons chopped flat-leaf parsley
2 tablespoons chopped fresh dill or chives
¹/₄ cup finely diced seeded tomato

Serve this mounded on cucumber rounds, rye toast, crumpets, or blinis, or for a low-calorie accompaniment, experiment with apple or pear slices.

1. In a small saucepan, heat ¹/₄ cup of the broth. Pour into a medium mixing bowl.

2. Sprinkle the gelatin over the broth. Let sit for 1 minute, then stir to dissolve the gelatin completely and set aside.

3. In a small saucepan, combine the lemon juice and zest, cayenne, and remaining stock and bring to a boil over high heat. Remove from the heat.

4. Add to the gelatin mixture and stir to combine. Refrigerate until the gelatin begins to thicken but is not set, about 15 minutes.

5. Add the shrimp, parsley, dill or chives, and tomato to the gelatin mixture. Stir gently to mix well.

6. Transfer the mixture to a terrine or individual ramekins. Cover with plastic wrap and refrigerate until the gelatin is completely set and the mixture is firm, 1 hour or more. Serve chilled.

Variation

Instead of shrimp, use cooked and chopped rock shrimp, crab, lobster tail, sea scallops, or trout fillets.

Process until smooth.

Crab Louis Topper

Makes about 3 cups

Surround a bowl of this classic topper with endive spears, and fill a basket with an assortment of crisp crackers, such as water crackers or standard saltines.

1 pound fresh lump crabmeat, picked clean of any shell pieces, meat broken apart with a fork, and drained
$^1/_3$ cup finely diced red bell pepper
$^1/_3$ cup finely diced green bell pepper
$^1/_3$ cup finely diced celery
$1^1/_2$ tablespoons lime juice
$^1/_4$ cup dry vermouth or white wine
$^2/_3$ cup mayonnaise, regular or low-fat, or equal parts of yogurt and sour cream, regular or low-fat
3 tablespoons bottled spicy cocktail sauce, or Tomato Chutney (see page 86)
2 scallions, white and some green parts, finely chopped
Grated zest of 1 lemon or lime
$^1/_4$ teaspoon Tabasco
Salt
Freshly ground white pepper

1. In a medium mixing bowl, combine the crab, peppers, celery, 1 tablespoon of the lime juice, and all but 1 tablespoon of the vermouth or wine. Toss to mix well and set aside.

2. In another mixing bowl, combine the mayonnaise or yogurt and sour cream mixture, the sauce or chutney, scallions, lemon or lime zest, Tabasco, remaining lime juice, and remaining wine. Blend well with a fork.

3. Pour the mayonnaise mixture over the crab mixture and toss to mix well. Season to taste with salt and white pepper. Press into a serving dish. Cover with plastic wrap and chill before serving.

Thai Shrimp Topper

Makes about 1³/₄ cups

1/2 cup dried shrimp (see Note)
2 small Japanese eggplants, ends trimmed
1/2 clove garlic, finely chopped
1 teaspoon grated fresh ginger
1/4 cup fish sauce (nam pla; see Note)
1/4 cup fresh lemon or lime juice
1 tablespoon sugar, or more to taste
1 tablespoon dark sesame oil
2 tablespoons sesame seeds

1. In a small bowl, combine the dried shrimp and enough warm water to cover. Let soak until soft, about 10 minutes. Drain and set aside.

2. Place the whole eggplants in a medium, heavy saucepan, cover with water, and bring to a boil. Reduce the heat to low and cook until tender, 20 to 25 minutes. Drain and rinse under cold running water to cool. Peel and coarsely chop.

3. Place the eggplant in the bowl of a food processor fitted with the metal blade. Add the shrimp, garlic, ginger, fish sauce, lemon or lime juice, and sugar. Pulse to process until well combined. Add the sesame oil and process until a smooth consistency forms. Transfer to a serving bowl, sprinkle with the sesame seeds, and serve at room temperature.

Note: Dried shrimp and fish sauce (nam pla) can be found in Asian food markets.

Serve this exotic combination with a selection of Asian vegetables, including snow-pea pods, fresh shiitake mushroom pieces, long curly green beans, and very thin Japanese eggplant slices.

Tomato Sardine Tapenade

Makes about 1¹/₄ cups

Serve with celery sticks, endive spears, crisp toast, or crackers.

4 sardine fillets, drained, trimmed of skin and bones, and chopped
³/₄ cup black olive paste (see Note)
¹/₂ cup peeled, seeded, and diced plum tomatoes
¹/₂ teaspoon ground celery seed
Freshly ground black pepper
3 tablespoons chopped, pitted black olives

1. In a small bowl, mash the sardines with a fork. Add the olive paste, tomatoes, and celery seed and season to taste with ground pepper. Mash together. Add the chopped olives and stir to mix well.

2. Press into a crock or individual ramekins. Serve at room temperature.

Note: Olive paste is available in the deli section of most supermarkets.

Pineapple Salsa

Makes about 3 cups

1 large fresh pineapple, peeled, cored, and diced
$^1/_4$ cup chopped red bell pepper
1 small serrano or jalapeño chile, seeded, deveined, and finely chopped
  (see page xiv)
2 shallots, or $^1/_2$ small red onion, finely chopped
2 tablespoons fresh lime juice
2 tablespoons finely chopped cilantro
Pinch of salt

1. In a medium pottery or glass bowl, combine all the ingredients and stir to mix well.

2. Cover the bowl with plastic wrap and let marinate in the refrigerator for 1 hour. Served chilled.

Serve this along with turkey or chicken sausages, or grilled fish or chicken.

Sweet Onion and Raspberry Salsa

Makes about 2 cups

Serve this fresh, slightly sweet salsa on grilled fish, shrimp, or lobster.

1 sweet onion (Vidalia, Maui, or Walla Walla), finely diced
2 large ripe tomatoes, seeded and diced
1 yellow bell pepper, seeded and finely diced
1 poblano chile, roasted, peeled, seeded, deveined, and chopped (see page xiv)
1 tablespoon raspberry vinegar
2 tablespoons chopped cilantro or flat-leaf parsley
2 teaspoons extra virgin olive oil
2 cups chopped fresh raspberries, juice included
Salt
Freshly ground black pepper

1. In a medium pottery or glass bowl, combine the onion, tomatoes, bell pepper, poblano chile, vinegar, cilantro or parsley, and olive oil and stir to mix well. Fold in the raspberries and juice.

2. Season to taste with salt and pepper. Transfer to a serving bowl, cover with plastic wrap, and let marinate at room temperature for 1 hour.

3. Drain off most of the juice. Serve at room temperature.

Coconut Mango Topper

Makes about 2 cups

2 cups unsweetened coconut milk (see Note)

1 clove garlic, pressed

1 small serrano or jalapeño chile, seeded, deveined, and finely chopped
   (see page xiv), or to taste

2 large mangos, peeled, pitted, and diced

Juice of 2 limes

1/2 small sweet onion (Vidalia, Maui, or Walla Walla), chopped

4 scallions, white and some green parts, chopped

Pinch of ground ginger

Salt

Freshly ground white pepper

3 tablespoons finely chopped flat-leaf parsley or cilantro, or more to taste

1. In a small saucepan, combine the coconut milk, garlic, and chile and cook over low heat until reduced by half, about 15 minutes. Set aside to cool to room temperature.

2. In the bowl of a food processor fitted with the metal blade, place half the diced mangos and the lime juice and process to a purée. Add the coconut milk mixture, onion, scallions, and ginger. Pulse to combine, allowing some chunks to remain. Season to taste with salt and pepper. Stir in the parsley or cilantro and the remaining diced mangos.

3. Transfer to a serving bowl. Serve at room temperature, or cover with plastic wrap, refrigerate, and serve chilled.

Note: Canned coconut milk (not coconut syrup or coconut cream) is readily available in the specialty section of most supermarkets. A low-fat coconut milk that is now being shipped in from Hawaii is also suitable for this recipe.

Or make your own coconut milk: remove the meat of the coconut and cut off the brown outer coating. In a food processor, combine the coconut meat and 2 cups of very hot but not boiling water and process for about 2 minutes. Let sit for 2 to 3 minutes. Strain the coconut milk into a bowl, pressing the solids with the back of a wooden spoon. Discard the coconut solids.

Serve this hot-sweet topper with such hors d'oeuvres as grilled shellfish kebabs or grilled chicken satay. Consider marinating the fish or chicken in a citrus marinade before grilling.

Fresh Strawberry Chutney

Top fish or chicken with this sweet and slightly sour chutney. It even works as a topping for a very tart lemon cheesecake.

$^1/_2$ cup golden raisins, soaked in $^1/_2$ cup white wine for 1 hour
2 tablespoons honey
$^1/_2$ cup best-quality strawberry preserves
$^1/_4$ cup white wine vinegar
$^1/_3$ cup fresh orange juice
2 tablespoons fresh lemon juice
2 teaspoons ground ginger, or to taste
$^1/_8$ teaspoon cayenne pepper
1 medium navel orange, peeled, segmented, and chopped
6 cups whole strawberries, trimmed and chopped
$^1/_2$ cup chopped blanched almonds
1 tablespoon finely chopped fresh mint

1. Drain and chop the raisins, reserving $^1/_4$ cup of the wine.

2. In a large nonreactive saucepan, combine the raisins, reserved wine, honey, strawberry preserves, vinegar, orange juice, lemon juice, ginger, cayenne, and the orange. Bring to a boil, reduce the heat to medium, and cook, stirring frequently, until the liquid is thickened and syrupy, about 10 minutes.

3. Add the strawberries, cover partially, and continue cooking until the mixture is very thick, about 10 minutes more. Transfer to a bowl and let cool to room temperature.

4. Transfer to a serving dish, stir in the almonds and mint, and serve at room temperature. Or cover with plastic wrap, refrigerate, and serve chilled. Stir in the almonds and mint just before serving.

Variation

Sweet and Sour Strawberry Purée

At the end of step 3, after the ingredients have cooled, purée the strawberry mixture in a food processor fitted with the metal blade. Return to the saucepan and reduce by about $^1/_3$ over medium heat. Let cool to room temperature and stir in the mint but eliminate the nuts.

Apple, Raisin, and Green Tomato Chutney

Makes 2 cups

2 teaspoons extra virgin olive oil
2 cloves garlic, finely chopped
2 small leeks, white part only, separated, well washed, and finely chopped
3 to 4 medium green tomatoes, peeled, seeded (page xiv), and chopped
1 medium green bell pepper, seeded and finely chopped
Juice of 1 lime or lemon
1 green apple, peeled, cored, and finely diced
$1/4$ cup sugar, or 3 tablespoons honey
$1/4$ cup champagne vinegar or best-quality white wine vinegar
$1/2$ teaspoon salt
Pinch of freshly ground black pepper
1 teaspoon toasted, ground coriander seeds (see page xiv)
$1/4$ cup golden raisins (optional)
$1/4$ cup toasted sunflower seeds (see page xiv)

1. In a medium sauté pan, heat the olive oil over medium heat. Add the garlic and leeks and cook, stirring occasionally, until the leeks wilt, about 5 minutes.

2. Add the rest of the ingredients except the sunflower seeds. Continue cooking until the mixture is thick and syrupy, about 10 minutes.

3. Remove from the heat and let cool. Stir in the sunflower seeds, transfer to a serving dish, and serve at room temperature.

Here's a chutney that can be served with an assortment of spreads and toppers that offer contrasting flavors. Make a tasting-meal by offering this on a tray together with Smoked Salmon Fromage (page 144) and a cheese-and-wine spread (pages 15–20). For a few extra side dishes, include roasted potatoes, grilled chicken satay, and an assortment of breads and crackers.

Dips

Aioli-Garlic Mayonnaise Dip

Makes about 1 1/2 cups

1/4 teaspoon salt
6 to 10 cloves garlic, pressed
1 tablespoon fresh bread crumbs
2 large egg yolks
2 cups extra virgin olive oil
1 1/2 tablespoons fresh lemon juice

1. In the bowl of a food processor fitted with the metal blade, process the salt and garlic until well combined. Add the bread crumbs and process just to combine. Add the egg yolks and process to a well-combined paste.

2. With the motor of the food processor running, add a few drops of the olive oil and process to incorporate thoroughly. In a very thin stream, gradually continue adding the olive oil until it begins to thicken. After about half of the oil is totally incorporated, add the lemon juice. Continue adding oil only until the desired thickness has been achieved. (You may not need to use all of the oil.)

3. Transfer to a serving bowl. Serve immediately, or cover with plastic wrap, refrigerate, and serve chilled.

Variation

Spinach, Watercress, and Parsley

To the completed mayonnaise in the food processor, add 2 to 3 tablespoons finely chopped watercress leaves (blanched for 30 seconds and squeezed dry), 1/4 cup stemmed chopped fresh spinach leaves (blanched for 20 seconds and squeezed dry), and 2 tablespoons finely chopped flat-leaf parsley. Process to combine. Season to taste with salt and freshly ground black pepper.

Serve this as a dip for fresh vegetables or with cooked artichokes, crisp fresh vegetables, or shrimp. To create your own unique dips, mix with other ingredients, such as pesto, salsa, avocado, sun-dried tomatoes, or fresh herbs. Both mayonnaises can also be used as a sandwich spread.

Hot and Spicy Melted Butter Dip

Makes about 1 cup

Serve this peppery, hot-flavored butter dip with Roasted Curried Potato Wedges (page 160) instead of plain butter.

$^1/_4$ cup plus 2 tablespoons ($^3/_4$ stick) unsalted butter
1 clove garlic, pressed
1 small shallot, finely chopped
2 small jalapeño or serrano chilies, peeled, seeded, and finely chopped (see page xiv)
2 teaspoons finely chopped dry-packed sun-dried tomato
1 to 2 tablespoons chopped fresh herb of choice, such as thyme, flat-leaf parsley, or chives
Salt

1. In a small saucepan, melt the butter. Add the garlic, shallot, chilies, and sun-dried tomato and cook over very low heat until the shallot is tender but not browned, about 5 minutes.

2. Remove the pan from the heat and stir in the herbs. Season to taste with salt.

3. Serve in a chafing dish or transfer to a heatproof serving dish and place on an electric warming tray so the butter stays warm and does not harden.

Herb & Spice Pestos

Intense and full flavored, herb and spice pestos are especially delicious as a dip for Roasted Curried Potato Wedges (page 160), as a spread on grilled or broiled breads, as a raw vegetable vinaigrette dip (see Note), or as a topper for potato skins. Or combine pesto with other ingredients such as cream cheese for a flavorful cheese spread. Naturally flavorful, pestos can top off pasta, soups, grilled or broiled fish or chicken breasts.

Basic Herb Pesto

Makes $^1/_2$ to 1 cup

Packed fresh herb (see Variations)
$^1/_2$ **cup packed flat-leaf parsley**
1 cup packed spinach leaves (optional), well washed and dried
2 tablespoons pine nuts or other nuts (see Variations)
2 cloves garlic, pressed
$^1/_4$ **cup extra virgin olive oil**
2 tablespoons freshly grated Parmesan cheese

1. In a blender or the bowl of a food processor fitted with the metal blade, combine the herb, parsley, spinach if using, pine nuts, and garlic. Process until finely chopped.

2. With the motor running, add the oil in a thin but steady stream. Process until well blended. Stir in the Parmesan cheese.

3. Serve at room temperature. Or use as a flavoring in other spreads, toppers, and dips. Store in a tightly covered container in the refrigerator or freezer until needed.

Note: To make an instant vinaigrette dip, add more extra virgin olive oil to a pesto along with an acid such as lemon or other citrus juice, white wine vinegar, or red wine vinegar, to taste. Choose the acid that best compliments the flavors in the pesto.

(continued)

Variations

Thyme Pesto

Use $1/2$ cup packed fresh thyme.

Tarragon Pesto

Use $1/4$ cup loosely packed fresh tarragon.

Sage Pesto

Use $1/2$ cup loosely packed sage.

Oregano or Rosemary Pesto

Use $1/4$ cup finely chopped fresh oregano or rosemary for the herb, and $1/4$ cup toasted walnuts for the nuts.

Chive, Cilantro, or Dill Pesto

Use $1/4$ cup loosely packed chopped chives, $1 1/2$ cups loosely packed fresh cilantro, or 1 cup loosely packed fresh dill for herb; add 1 teaspoon lemon zest; and either use the pine nuts or substitute chopped blanched almonds or toasted walnuts.

Parsley and Nut Pesto

Use 2 additional cups parsley for the herbs and $1/2$ cup either pine nuts or toasted walnuts for the nuts. Substitute grated Romano for the Parmesan. Eliminate the spinach.

Provençal Mixed Herb Pesto

Use $1/4$ cup loosely packed of each herb: fresh tarragon, fresh oregano, fresh thyme, and fresh basil. Use 3 tablespoons pine nuts or pistachios for the nuts. Eliminate the spinach.

Classic Basil Pesto

Use 2 cups loosely packed fresh basil, $1/4$ cup pine nuts, and 3 tablespoons freshly grated Parmesan cheese. Eliminate the spinach.

Chipotle Chile Pesto

Makes about 2¹/₂ cups

3 to 4 cloves garlic, blanched for 2 minutes in boiling water
1 cup canned chipotle chilies (see Note), drained and trimmed
1¹/₂ ripe tomatoes, peeled, seeded, and finely chopped
1 tablespoon extra virgin olive oil
Salt
Freshly ground black pepper
1 tablespoon finely chopped toasted pumpkin seeds (see page xiv)

1. In the bowl of a food processor fitted with the metal blade, place the garlic cloves. Process until finely chopped. Scrape the sides of the bowl if necessary.

2. Add the chipotle chilies, tomatoes, and olive oil and process until only a very slight amount of chunky texture remains.

3. Transfer to a serving bowl and season with salt and pepper to taste. Stir in the pumpkin seeds and serve at room temperature. Or refrigerate in a tight-fitting glass jar until ready to use.

Note: Canned chipotle chilies are available in the Latin section of the grocery store or in Latin food markets.

The hot and smoky flavor of this pesto makes a wonderful addition to an assortment of dips, salsas, guacamole, and tortilla chips.

Basic Pesto Dip

Makes about 1 cup

Choose any of the highly flavored pestos in this chapter to make this quick dip. Serve with an assortment of fresh vegetables or chips.

1/4 cup plain yogurt, regular, low-fat, or nonfat
1/2 cup sour cream, regular, low-fat, or nonfat
1/4 to 1/2 cup pesto of choice (see pages 113–115)
1 teaspoon grated lemon zest, or more to taste
Salt
Freshly ground black pepper

1. In a medium bowl, combine the yogurt and sour cream. Stir in the pesto and lemon zest and season with salt and pepper to taste.

2. Transfer to a serving dish. Serve at room temperature, or cover with plastic wrap, refrigerate, and chill before serving.

Lemony Low-Fat Garbanzo Bean Dip

Makes about 1³/₄ cups

One 16-ounce can chickpeas (garbanzo beans), rinsed, drained, and patted dry
2 tablespoons fresh lemon juice, or more to taste
1 teaspoon grated lemon zest
¹/₂ cup firm tofu
¹/₂ cup nonfat sour cream
¹/₄ cup scallions, white and light green parts, chopped
¹/₂ teaspoon salt
¹/₂ teaspoon freshly ground black pepper

Serve this as a low-fat alternative to other bean dips. Pita chips make a perfect accompaniment.

1. In the bowl of a food processor fitted with the metal blade, combine the chickpeas, lemon juice and zest, tofu, sour cream, 3 tablespoons of the scallions, and the salt and pepper. Process to a light, fluffy consistency, leaving a slight amount of texture if desired.

2. Transfer to a small bowl. Sprinkle with the remaining scallions. Serve at room temperature, or cover with plastic wrap, refrigerate, and serve chilled.

Hummus

Makes about 2 1/2 cups

Serve this classic Middle Eastern dip with slices of pita or flatbread, crisp crackers, or vegetable slices such as zucchini or cucumber.

1 cup dried chickpeas (garbanzo beans)
1 teaspoon salt, plus more to taste
1/4 cup tahini, or to taste
1 to 2 cloves garlic, finely chopped
Juice of 1 lemon
1/2 teaspoon cayenne pepper
2 tablespoons extra virgin olive oil
3 tablespoons chopped flat-leaf parsley
1 teaspoon cumin or paprika for garnish

1. In a medium, heavy saucepan, place the chickpeas. Cover with enough water to reach 2 inches above the top of the beans. Bring to a boil, lower the heat to medium, and cook 5 minutes. Remove from the heat, cover partially, and let stand for 1 hour.

2. Drain the chickpeas and rinse under running water. Clean the saucepan and return the chickpeas. Add 1 teaspoon of salt and the 4 cups of water, cover, and bring to a boil. Reduce the heat to low and cook until tender, about 1 hour.

3. Drain, reserving the liquid, and transfer the chickpeas to the bowl of a food processor fitted with the metal blade. Process to a smooth paste. Add the tahini, garlic, and lemon juice and pulse to mix, using the reserved liquid as needed until a smooth, spreadable consistency forms. Season to taste with salt and cayenne.

4. Place in a shallow serving dish, drizzle with the olive oil, and swirl the oil into the top of the hummus slightly but do not mix in. Sprinkle with the parsley and dust with the cumin or paprika. Serve at room temperature.

Variations

Low-Fat Hummus

Substitute chicken broth for the water when cooking the dried chickpeas. Reduce the tahini to 1 tablespoon and add 1 to 2 tablespoons toasted sesame seeds (see page xiv) to the food processor. Sprinkle the top with chopped parsley and more toasted sesame seeds if desired.

Quick Hummus

Substitute 3 cups well-drained canned chickpeas and begin at step 3.

Cilantro Hummus

Substitute $1/4$ cup chopped cilantro for the parsley. Serve with Herb or Spice Pita Chips (page 162).

Lentil Hummus

Substitute red or brown lentils for the chickpeas. Cook the lentils until tender, about 25 to 30 minutes, in chicken or vegetable broth instead of water before processing with the other ingredients.

Creamy Refried Bean Dip

Makes about 3 cups

A can of refried beans is the basis for this quick and tasty Mexican-style bean dip. It's great with tortilla or pita chips.

2 cups canned refried beans
$^1/_3$ cup sour cream, regular or low-fat
$1^1/_2$ teaspoons ground cumin
$^2/_3$ cup Spicy Fresh Tomato Salsa (page 80) or
   Tomato Poblano Salsa (page 84)
Pinch of salt
Pinch of freshly ground black pepper

1. In the bowl of a food processor fitted with the metal blade, place the beans and pulse a few times to form a slightly textured consistency. Add the sour cream, cumin, and $^1/_2$ cup of the salsa and pulse to combine, leaving some chunks of tomato visible, or process to a smooth consistency if desired.

2. Stir in the remaining salsa. Season to taste with salt and pepper.

3. Transfer to a serving bowl. Serve at room temperature.

Variation

Warm Bean Dip with Jack Cheese

Preheat the oven to 225°F. Substitute $^1/_2$ cup grated Jack cheese for the sour cream. Place the dip in a shallow flameproof dish and place in the oven until warmed through, about 10 minutes. The consistency should be slightly runny. Turn on the broiler, top the dip with 2 tablespoons of grated Jack cheese, and place under the broiler until the cheese bubbles but is not brown, 1 to 2 minutes. Serve immediately.

Curried Red Lentil Dip

Makes about 3 cups

1³/₄ cups dried red lentils, washed and drained
2 teaspoons salt
1 teaspoon ground turmeric
2 teaspoons crushed red pepper flakes
4 cups water, or more as needed
One 1-inch piece fresh ginger, peeled
3 cloves garlic, chopped
1 large onion, quartered
2 tablespoons unsalted butter
2 medium tomatoes, peeled, seeded, and finely chopped
1¹/₂ teaspoons mild or hot curry powder (Madras or best quality available),
   or to taste
3 tablespoons plain yogurt, regular or low-fat
2 tablespoons chopped cilantro

Serve this Indian-style dip with the traditional naan (Indian flatbread) or with warmed pita slices.

1. In a medium, heavy saucepan, combine the lentils, 1 teaspoon of the salt, the turmeric, red pepper flakes, and water. Add more water as needed to cover the lentils. Bring to a boil, reduce the heat to low, and cook until the lentils are tender, 10 to 12 minutes. Skim the surface of scum if necessary during cooking. Place in a strainer; rinse and drain well.

2. Meanwhile, in the bowl of a food processor fitted with the metal blade or in a blender, process the ginger, garlic, and onion until minced.

3. In a medium skillet or sauté pan, melt the butter over medium heat. Add the ginger mixture and cook over low heat for 4 minutes. Add the tomatoes and curry powder and continue cooking for 3 minutes more. Add the lentils and the remaining 1 teaspoon of salt and cook 3 minutes more. Cool slightly.

4. Transfer the lentil mixture to the food processor bowl and process to a smooth paste. Stir in the yogurt to mix well. Transfer to a serving dish and sprinkle with the cilantro. Serve at room temperature.

Thai Peanut Dip

Makes about 1 1/2 cups

Serve this Thai-influenced dip with grilled marinated chicken, beef satay sticks, and other Asian appetizers. It also makes a classic peanut sauce when tossed into cooked pasta or soba noodles and finished with a sprinkling of chopped, unsalted, roasted peanuts and scallion greens.

1/2 cup crunchy peanut butter
1/2 cup unsweetened coconut milk (see Note)
2 tablespoons tamarind concentrate (see Note)
1 tablespoon Thai fish sauce (nam pla; see Note)
1 clove garlic, minced
One 1 1/4-inch piece ginger, peeled and minced
1 tablespoon packed dark brown sugar, or 2 teaspoons honey
1 stalk lemongrass, bottom 3 or 4 inches only, tough outer leaves removed, minced (see Note)
1/4 cup very hot water
1 teaspoon chili oil (see Note)

1. In a small glass or pottery mixing bowl, combine the peanut butter, coconut milk, and tamarind concentrate and stir to mix. Add the remaining ingredients except the chili oil and hot water and mix well.

2. Add the water 1 tablespoon at a time, mixing well before each addition. Stir in the chili oil. Transfer to a serving bowl and serve at room temperature.

Note: These ingredients are available at Asian food markets and in the Asian ingredients section of supermarkets. For directions on making your own coconut milk, see page 105.

Toasted Pumpkin Seed
and Parsley Dip

Makes about 1 1/2 cups

3/4 cup plain yogurt, regular, low-fat, or nonfat
3/4 cup cottage cheese, regular or low-fat
3 tablespoons fresh lemon juice
1 teaspoon grated lemon zest
2 cloves garlic, pressed
Pinch of ground cumin or coriander
1 cup toasted unsalted pumpkin seeds (see page xiv)
2/3 cup finely chopped flat-leaf parsley or cilantro
Salt
Freshly ground black pepper

Serve this dip with raw, blanched, or grilled vegetables or with crackers.

1. In the bowl of a food processor fitted with the metal blade or in a blender, combine the yogurt, cottage cheese, lemon juice and zest, garlic, and cumin or coriander. Process to a smooth consistency.

2. Add 3/4 cup of the pumpkin seeds and all but 1 tablespoon of the parsley and pulse a few times just to combine, leaving pieces of pumpkin seed visible.

3. Season to taste with salt and pepper. Transfer to a serving bowl and top with the remaining pumpkin seeds and parsley. Serve at room temperature.

Toasted Sesame Seed Dip
(Tahini Dip)

Makes about 1 1/4 cups

This matches well with warmed pita wedges.

1/3 cup tahini
3 tablespoons fresh lemon juice
1/4 teaspoon grated lemon zest
1 cup plain yogurt, regular, low-fat, or nonfat
1 clove garlic, pressed
1 tablespoon finely chopped flat-leaf parsley or scallion (dark green part)
Pinch of salt
Pinch of cayenne
2 tablespoons toasted sesame seeds (see page xiv)

1. In the bowl of a food processor fitted with the metal blade or in a blender, combine the tahini, lemon juice and zest, yogurt, and garlic. Process to a smooth consistency.

2. Stir in the parsley or scallion greens, salt, cayenne, and all but 1 teaspoon of the sesame seeds.

3. Transfer to a serving bowl and sprinkle with the remaining sesame seeds. Serve at room temperature, or cover with plastic wrap, refrigerate, and serve chilled.

Variation

Reduce 1/4 cup of orange juice to 2 tablespoons over medium heat and use in place of 2 tablespoons of the lemon juice. Or instead of plain yogurt, substitute Yogurt Cheese (page 28) for a thicker consistency.

Cheese, Cream, & Yogurt Dips

Classic Blue Cheese Dip

Makes about 2 cups

¹/₂ **pound blue-veined cheese, such as domestic blue cheese or imported gorgonzola or Roquefort, plus 2 tablespoons crumbled**
¹/₄ **cup plus 1 tablespoon mayonnaise, regular or reduced-calorie**
¹/₄ **cup plus 1 tablespoon sour cream, regular or low-fat**
2 tablespoons white wine vinegar
2 tablespoons milk
Salt
Freshly ground white pepper

1. In the bowl of a food processor fitted with the metal blade, combine the ¹/₂ pound of blue cheese, the mayonnaise, sour cream, vinegar, and milk. Process to a smooth purée.

2. Season to taste with salt and pepper. Stir in the 2 tablespoons of crumbled blue cheese.

3. Transfer to a serving dish and serve at room temperature, or cover with plastic wrap, refrigerate, and serve chilled.

Serve this popular standard with blanched broccoli or cauliflower florets, Belgian endive, or romaine lettuce spears, or top Potato Skins (page 172) or dip in with Roasted Curried Potato Wedges (page 160).

Real Ranch Dip

Makes about 2 1/2 cups

If you like ranch salad dressing, then you'll love this creamy, made-from-scratch dip. Surround a bowl with blanched raw vegetables, well-chilled romaine lettuce leaves, or even freshly made French fries.

1 cup mayonnaise, regular or reduced-calorie, or a combination of low-fat cottage cheese and nonfat yogurt
1 cup sour cream, regular or low-fat
1 cup buttermilk, low-fat or nonfat
3 tablespoons chopped flat-leaf parsley
2 teaspoons white wine vinegar
1 tablespoon minced onion, or 1 teaspoon onion powder
1/2 small clove garlic, minced, or 1/2 teaspoon garlic powder
1/2 teaspoon salt
1/4 teaspoon freshly ground black pepper

1. In a blender or the bowl of a food processor fitted with the metal blade, combine all the ingredients and process to mix well.

2. Transfer to a serving container, cover with plastic wrap, refrigerate, and serve chilled.

Spinach and Crunchy Chopped Veggie Dip

Makes about 2$^1/_2$ cups

2 teaspoons extra virgin olive oil
2 shallots, finely chopped
1 pound fresh spinach, stemmed, well washed, and patted dry
   with paper towels
$^1/_4$ cup freshly grated Parmesan cheese
1 cup ricotta, regular or part-skim, drained
Pinch of ground nutmeg
Pinch of cayenne pepper
Salt
Freshly ground black pepper
$^1/_2$ cup diced carrots, blanched
$^1/_4$ cup diced radishes
$^1/_4$ cup finely chopped celery
$^1/_4$ cup finely chopped fresh jicama (see Note)
$^1/_4$ cup finely chopped zucchini

1. In a large nonstick skillet or sauté pan, heat the olive oil over medium heat. Add the shallots and cook until tender, 2 to 3 minutes. Lower the heat, add the spinach, cover the pan, and let wilt for about 1 minute. Transfer to a colander or fine-mesh strainer to drain and cool. Press lightly with the back of a wooden spoon to remove any moisture.

2. Transfer the spinach mixture to the bowl of a food processor fitted with the metal blade and process to a purée. Add the Parmesan, ricotta, nutmeg, and cayenne and pulse to combine well. Season to taste with salt and pepper. Stir in the remaining ingredients. Do not process further.

3. Transfer to a serving dish. Serve at room temperature, or cover with plastic wrap, refrigerate, and serve chilled.

Note: Jicama is grown mainly in Mexico. It's a large root vegetable similar to a potato and has a moist, sweet taste and crisp, crunchy texture.

This is a fresh, homemade version of a standard party dip that is usually made with sour cream and dehydrated vegetable soup mix. What a difference this delicious dip makes. Serve it with a combination of Homemade Vegetable Chips (page 168).

Roasted Sweet Red Pepper Dip

Makes about 2 cups

This versatile dip is not only creamy and light but also low in calories, as the recipe calls for low-fat cream cheese and sour cream. Serve it with Chinese appetizers, grilled chicken satay sticks, or other finger foods.

1/4 cup plus 1 tablespoon Roasted Garlic Purée (page 3)
3 red bell peppers, roasted, peeled, and seeded (see page xiv)
1/2 teaspoon ground cumin
1/2 cup nonfat cream cheese
1/2 cup low-fat cream cheese
2 tablespoons low-fat sour cream or crème fraîche (see page 44)
Salt
Freshly ground white pepper

1. In the bowl of a food processor fitted with the metal blade, combine the garlic purée, peppers, and cumin and process to a smooth purée.

2. Add the cream cheese and process until completely incorporated. Stir in the sour cream or crème fraîche. Season to taste with salt and pepper.

3. Transfer to a serving dish and serve at room temperature, or cover with plastic wrap, refrigerate, and serve chilled.

Quick Creamy Pesto Dip

Makes about 3 cups

**1 cup packed fresh basil leaves, chopped, plus 1 tablespoon for garnish
(see Note)**
1 clove garlic, pressed
1 cup freshly grated Parmesan cheese
1¹/₂ cups low-fat cream cheese or plain Yogurt Cheese (page 28)
2 tablespoons milk, or more as needed
Salt
Freshly ground black pepper, plus 4 to 6 turns of the peppermill for garnish

1. In the bowl of a food processor fitted with the metal blade, process the basil and garlic until finely chopped.

2. Add the Parmesan and cream cheese or yogurt cheese and process to a smooth consistency. Add the milk a little at a time until the desired consistency is reached. Season to taste with salt and pepper.

3. Transfer to a serving bowl and top with several turns of the peppermill. Serve immediately.

Note: If you have basil pesto on hand, use ¹/₂ to ³/₄ cup, or to taste, in place of the basil leaves, garlic, and Parmesan cheese.

Almost any finger food goes great with this classic pesto dip, from chips, flatbreads, and grilled bread, to tiny pancakes or blinis, to crispy croûtes, potato skins, and tempura vegetables (see page xxiii).

Indian Raita Dip

Makes about 1 1/2 cups

Serve this spicy and flavorful yogurt dip with puri (the flatbread of India) or other Middle Eastern flatbread. Many health food emporiums now carry a large selection of both regular and fat-reduced flatbreads.

1 clove garlic, minced
1 cup plain nonfat yogurt or Spicy Yogurt Topper (page 67)
1 hothouse cucumber, peeled, halved lengthwise, seeded, thinly sliced crosswise, drained in a strainer for 20 minutes, and patted dry with paper towels
1/2 small red onion, halved and thinly sliced
2 scallions, white and some green parts, chopped separately
Salt
Freshly ground pepper
1 tablespoon toasted poppy seeds or onion seeds (see page xiv)

1. In a medium mixing bowl, combine the garlic, yogurt, cucumber, all but 2 teaspoons of the red onion, the white part of the scallion, and stir to mix well. Season to taste with salt and pepper. Marinate at room temperature for 1 to 2 hours.

2. Transfer to a serving bowl and sprinkle with the toasted seeds, the remaining red onion, and the green part of the scallion. Serve at room temperature, or cover with plastic wrap, refrigerate, and serve chilled.

Low-Fat Tofu Yogurt Dip

Makes about 1 cup

1/2 cup firm tofu
1/2 cup nonfat yogurt or cottage cheese
1 tablespoon fresh lemon juice
1 teaspoon grated lemon zest
2 scallions, white and light green parts chopped separately
Salt
Freshly ground black pepper

1. In the bowl of a food processor fitted with the metal blade, combine the tofu, yogurt or cottage cheese, lemon juice and zest, and white part of the scallion, and process until well combined and light and fluffy. Season to taste with salt and pepper. Stir in the green part of the scallion.

2. Transfer to a serving bowl and serve immediately. Or cover with plastic wrap, refrigerate, and serve chilled.

Serve this low-fat dip with a basket of raw or blanched vegetables to make a pre-barbecue crudité platter. Add a few tablespoons of chopped fresh herbs, or heighten the flavor with a homemade pesto (pages 113–116) or tapenade (pages 14, 62, 63, and 102). Exchange the yogurt for nonfat cottage cheese if desired. A chopped vine-ripened tomato makes a tasty and colorful addition. This dip is versatile—use your imagination.

Baba Ghanouj
(Middle Eastern Eggplant Dip)

Makes about 1 1/2 cups

Serve this with fresh vegetables, Rustic Croûtes (pages 152–153), warm slices of pita, or Herb or Spice Pita Chips (page 162).

1 large eggplant, halved lengthwise, baked cut-side down in a 350°F oven for 1 hour, and flesh scooped out
1 clove garlic, pressed
$1/3$ cup fresh lemon juice
$1/4$ cup tahini
1 tablespoon extra virgin olive oil
$1/8$ teaspoon ground cumin
Salt
Freshly ground black pepper
2 tablespoons chopped flat-leaf parsley

1. In the bowl of a food processor fitted with the metal blade, process the eggplant to a coarse consistency.

2. Add the garlic, lemon juice, tahini, olive oil, and cumin. Process just to mix. Season to taste with salt and pepper. Stir in the parsley.

3. Transfer to a serving bowl. Serve at room temperature.

Provençal Eggplant Spread

Makes about 1 1/2 cups

1 large eggplant, halved lengthwise, baked cut-side down in a 350°F oven for
   1 hour, and flesh scooped out
2 cloves garlic, minced
2 flat anchovy fillets, drained and finely chopped, or more to taste
2 tablespoons extra virgin olive oil
Salt
Freshly ground black pepper

This pairs nicely with Rustic Croûtes (pages 152–153) or slices of country-style bread.

1. In the bowl of a food processor fitted with the metal blade, process the eggplant to a coarse consistency.

2. Add the garlic and anchovies and process just to mix. With the motor running, add the olive oil in a thin but steady stream and continue processing until light and fluffy. Season to taste with salt and pepper.

3. Transfer to a serving bowl. Serve at room temperature.

Scallion, Yogurt Cheese, and Eggplant Dip

Makes about 1 1/2 cups

Thanks to Anita Gottehrer for this wonderful, summery, low-fat dip. She suggests serving it with an assortment of fresh vegetables or sesame thins.

1 large eggplant, halved lengthwise, baked cut-side down in a 350°F oven for 1 hour, and flesh scooped out
1 cup Yogurt Cheese (page 28)
2 tablespoons fresh lemon juice
3 cloves garlic, finely chopped
3 tablespoons chopped fresh dill
2 cups finely chopped scallions, white and some green parts
1 tablespoon minced jalapeño chile, or more to taste
3 tablespoons extra virgin olive oil
Salt
Freshly ground black pepper
2 tablespoons toasted sesame seeds (see page xiv)

1. In the bowl of a food processor fitted with the metal blade, process the eggplant to a coarse consistency.

2. Add the yogurt cheese, lemon juice, garlic, dill, scallions, and jalapeño. Process just to mix. With the motor running, add the olive oil in a thin but steady stream until completely incorporated. Season to taste with salt and pepper.

3. Transfer to a serving bowl. Cover with plastic wrap, refrigerate, and serve chilled. Top with sesame seeds just before serving.

Quick Guacamole

Makes 1¹/₂ cups

3 medium ripe Haas avocados, halved, pitted, and flesh scooped out
Juice of 1 lime, plus 1 tablespoon
2 to 3 cloves garlic, minced
4 scallions, white part only, chopped
¹/₂ cup finely chopped cilantro
1 small jalapeño chile, seeded, deveined, and minced (see page xiv)

1. In a medium mixing bowl, mash the avocado with a fork to achieve a partially smooth and partially chunky consistency.

2. Stir in the juice of 1 lime, garlic, scallions, cilantro, and jalapeño and mix well.

3. Transfer to a serving dish. Sprinkle the top with the remaining 1 tablespoon lime juice. Serve immediately.

Serve this quick and easy dip with chips of any type, including blue or yellow corn chips or Homemade Vegetable Chips (page 168). Look for baked, not fried, tortilla chips, which are now available in most markets.

Tomato Guacamole

Makes about 1 1/2 cups

Serve this fresh avocado dip with the new commercially made baked tortilla chips. These are lower in fat and calories and are crisper and more delicate than fried tortilla chips. The white corn baked chips go especially well with this type of guacamole. Another interesting match-up is Crispy Won Ton Strips (page 173).

2 medium ripe Haas avocados, halved, pitted, and flesh scooped out
Juice of 1 lime or lemon, plus 1 tablespoon
2 cloves garlic, minced
1/3 cup coarsely chopped white onion
1 small jalapeño or serrano chile, seeded, deveined (see page xiv), and minced
1 tablespoon finely chopped cilantro
1/3 cup peeled, seeded, and diced tomato
Pinch of salt
Pinch of freshly ground white pepper

1. In a medium mixing bowl, mash the avocado with a fork to achieve a partially smooth and partially chunky consistency.

2. Stir in all but 1 tablespoon of the lime or lemon juice, the garlic, onion, jalapeño, cilantro, and tomato, and mix well. Add the salt and pepper.

3. Transfer to a serving dish. Sprinkle the top with the remaining lime or lemon juice and serve immediately.

Orange Guacamole

Makes about 1 $^1/_2$ cups

2 medium ripe Haas avocados, halved, pitted, and flesh scooped out, half
    mashed and half diced
Juice of 1 lemon
Grated zest of 1 lemon
1 medium navel orange, peeled, segmented, well trimmed, and chopped
$^1/_4$ cup finely chopped red onion
$^1/_2$ teaspoon crushed red pepper flakes, or more to taste
Pinch of ground cinnamon
1 tablespoon tequila
2 tablespoons finely chopped cilantro or flat-leaf parsley
Salt
Freshly ground white pepper

1. In a small bowl, combine the mashed part of the avocado, the
lemon juice and zest, chopped orange, red onion, pepper flakes, cinnamon, and tequila. Stir to mix well.

2. Stir in the diced avocado, and cilantro or parsley. Season to taste
with salt and pepper.

3. Transfer to a serving dish. Serve immediately.

Variation

Grapefruit Guacamole

*Substitute a small ruby red sweet grapefruit for the orange, and add a
teaspoon of sugar to the guacamole if desired.*

Serve this unique version of the classic with Crispy Won Ton Strips (page 173), celery heart stalks, or even calorie-saving lettuce cups, which can be filled with guacamole and rolled up.

Pacific Rim Guacamole

Makes about 1 1/2 cups

Instead of serving with tortilla chips, pair this Hawaiian-Japanese fusion guacamole with Terra Chips (available in health food stores) or Japanese crunchy rice cakes.

2 ripe large Haas avocados, halved, pitted, and flesh scooped out
3 tablespoons plain yogurt, regular or low-fat
2 teaspoons wasabi powder (see Note)
1/4 cup pickled ginger (see Note), well drained and roughly chopped
12 scallions, white and some green parts, finely chopped
2 tablespoons toasted sesame seeds (see page xiv)
2 tablespoons fresh lime juice
1 teaspoon grated lime zest
Salt
Freshly ground black pepper

1. In a medium pottery or glass mixing bowl, mash the avocados with a fork to achieve a partially smooth and partially chunky consistency.

2. In a small pottery or glass mixing bowl, whisk the yogurt and wasabi together. Make sure the wasabi is completely incorporated by pressing any small lumps into the yogurt with the back of a spoon.

3. To the avocados, add the yogurt mixture, the ginger, scallions, sesame seeds, lime juice, and zest and stir to mix well. Season to taste with salt and pepper.

4. Transfer to a pottery or glass serving dish and serve immediately. Or sprinkle the top of the guacamole with more lime juice, cover with plastic wrap, making sure the wrap is touching the top of the guacamole, refrigerate, and serve chilled.

Note: These ingredients are available in the Asian section of the supermarket or a Japanese food market.

Garlic and Bell Pepper Guacamole

Makes 1 1/2 cups

1 large ripe Haas avocado, halved, pitted, and flesh scooped out
1 small yellow bell pepper, roasted, peeled (see page xiv), and diced
1 small red bell pepper, roasted, peeled (see page xiv), and diced
1 cup seeded and diced ripe tomato
2 scallions, white and some green parts, chopped
Juice of 1 lime
1/2 teaspoon chili powder, or 1/8 teaspoon cayenne pepper
2 tablespoons Roasted Garlic Purée (page 3)
Salt

1. In a small pottery or glass mixing bowl, mash the avocado with a fork to a smooth paste. Add all the peppers, tomato, and scallions, all but 1 tablespoon of the lime juice, the chili powder or cayenne, and the garlic purée and stir to mix well. Season to taste with salt.

2. Transfer to a glass or pottery serving bowl. Swirl in the remaining lime juice. Serve immediately, or cover with plastic wrap, making sure the wrap touches the top so it won't turn dark, refrigerate, and serve chilled.

This type of guacamole has a slightly sweeter characteristic than the classic Mexican style. Serve it with vegetable crudités, an assortment of Homemade Vegetable Chips (page 168), or crackers.

Spicy Bell Pepper Purée

Makes about 1 $^1/_2$ cups

Serve this dip with
Chinese potstickers or
blanched vegetables,
or even add a dollop
to a baked potato.

3 red bell peppers, roasted, peeled, seeded (see page xiv), and roughly
   chopped
$^1/_2$ green bell pepper, seeded and chopped
1 fresh jalapeño or other hot green chile, roasted, deveined, seeded,
   and chopped (see page xiv)
2 tablespoons extra virgin olive oil
2 tablespoons fresh lime or lemon juice
Pinch of salt
Pinch of sugar

1. In the bowl of a food processor fitted with the metal blade, combine all the bell peppers and the jalapeño and process to a purée.

2. Add the olive oil and the lime or lemon juice and process just
to mix. Add the salt and sugar.

3. Transfer to a serving bowl. Serve at room temperature.

Fresh Tomato and Miso Dip

Makes about 4 cups

6 large tomatoes (about 3 pounds), cored and quartered
1 tablespoon finely chopped peeled fresh ginger
$^1/_2$ cup rice vinegar
3 tablespoons maple syrup
$^1/_4$ cup light-colored miso paste (see Note)
$^1/_4$ teaspoon salt
$^1/_4$ teaspoon freshly ground black pepper
$1^1/_4$ teaspoons olive oil
2 tablespoons finely chopped fresh basil

Serve this as a dip for raw vegetables. To make a thicker, creamy dip, add Yogurt Cheese (page 28) or blended cottage cheese.

1. In the bowl of a food processor fitted with the metal blade, combine the tomatoes and ginger. Process to a smooth consistency.

2. Pour through a fine-mesh sieve or strainer into a medium nonreactive saucepan. Discard the remaining solids. Cook over medium-high heat until reduced to about one-third the original amount. Transfer to a bowl and let cool to room temperature.

3. Stir in the vinegar, maple syrup, miso, salt, pepper, and mix well. Cover with plastic wrap and refrigerate for 1 hour.

4. Transfer to a serving dish, stir in the olive oil and basil. Serve immediately.

Note: Miso is readily available in health food stores or the Asian or soup section of some grocery stores.

Seafood Dips

Creamy Anchovy Dip

Makes about 2 cups

Serve this full-flavored dip with crisp crackers, bread sticks, or raw vegetables such as blanched snow peas or Belgian endive spears.

Two 2-ounce cans flat anchovy fillets, drained, excess oil wiped off
    with paper towel, and chopped
2 cloves garlic, pressed
$1/_4$ cup water
$1^1/_2$ cups sour cream
2 tablespoons fresh lemon juice
Freshly ground black pepper

1. In a small skillet, combine the anchovies, garlic, water, and $1/_4$ cup of the sour cream. Bring to a boil, reduce the heat to low and cook, stirring occasionally, until very thick, about 10 minutes.

2. In the bowl of a food processor fitted with the metal blade, combine the anchovy mixture, remaining sour cream, and lemon juice, and process until smooth. Season to taste with pepper.

3. Transfer to a serving bowl, cover with plastic wrap, refrigerate for at least 1 hour, and serve chilled.

Taramasalata

Makes about 2 cups

4 slices white bread, crusts removed
$^1/_2$ cup tarama (see Note)
1 onion, roughly chopped
$^1/_4$ cup extra virgin olive oil
2 to 4 tablespoons fresh lemon juice
$^1/_4$ cup sour cream, regular or low-fat, or crème fraîche (see page 44)
2 tablespoons chopped flat-leaf parsley
2 olive oil-cured dried black olives, pitted and chopped

1. In a small bowl, place the bread slices with just enough water to dampen completely. Squeeze out any excess water. Transfer to the bowl of a food processor fitted with the metal blade.

2. Add the tarama and onion and pulse just to mix. With the motor running, add the olive oil in a thin but steady stream and process until incorporated. Then add the lemon juice in a thin but steady stream and process until completely incorporated.

3. Transfer to a serving bowl, fold in the sour cream or crème fraîche, cover with plastic wrap, and refrigerate until well chilled. Sprinkle with the parsley and olives before serving.

Note: Tarama, pale orange carp roe, is available in jars in the cold deli section of the supermarket. In place of tarama, you can use mullet, salmon, or smoked cod roe.

Serve this light but full-flavored Greek specialty made with tarama, or carp roe, as a cocktail-time hors d'oeuvre dip with slices of pita or crusty country-style bread. Or make an entire tasting-meal by adding it to an assortment of hors d'oeuvres that includes scallions and kalamata olives, pieces of fresh feta cheese, Skordalia (a Greek garlic dip, page 56), celery, cucumber slices, and even traditional anise-flavored drinks like ouzo or Pernod.

Smoked Salmon Fromage

Makes about 2 cups

Fromage blanc is a goat cheese curd whipped to a creamy texture. Its fresh taste when mixed with smoked salmon makes a perfect pairing of flavors and a light consistency, great for dipping crusty French bread slices, thinly sliced pumpernickel bread, crackers, or crudités. It's elegant.

1¹/₂ cups fromage blanc or Montrachet chèvre (see page 23)
3 tablespoons chopped fresh chives
2 cloves garlic, peeled and minced
4 ounces smoked salmon, flaked or roughly chopped
Pinch of freshly ground white pepper

1. In a medium bowl, using a wooden spoon, lightly mix together the fromage blanc or chèvre, chives, and garlic until fluffy.

2. Fold in the salmon and add the white pepper. Place in a serving dish, cover with plastic wrap, refrigerate, and serve chilled.

Banana Ricotta Cream Dip

Makes about 2 1/2 cups

4 bananas, frozen and peeled (bananas should not be frozen solid
  but slightly soft, so that they flake with a fork)
2 cups part-skim ricotta, drained
1/4 cup cream cheese, regular or low-fat, at room temperature
2 tablespoons sugar or honey
2 teaspoons vanilla extract
2 teaspoons grated lemon zest

1. In the bowl of a food processor fitted with the metal blade, process the bananas into small chunks. Transfer to a bowl and set aside.

2. Do not wash the bowl of the food processor. Add the rest of the ingredients and process until well blended. Return the bananas to the food processor and pulse to process until smooth. Some flecks of icy banana will remain.

3. Transfer to a serving dish and serve immediately. Or set the serving dish in a bowl of ice on a buffet table to keep cold.

Surround the serving bowl with an assortment of slightly sweet breads and crackers, such as raisin pumpernickel bread, anise or almond biscotti, or crisp chocolate wafers.

Cinnamon Honey Yogurt Dip

Makes about 1¹/₂ cups

Serve this as a dip with almost any type of fresh fruit slices. Or make fruit kebabs of apple, pear, peach, and pineapple pieces to serve alongside individual servings of the dip for dessert. Also try dipping graham crackers and chocolate wafers into this pleasantly sweet and spicy combination of flavors.

1¹/₂ cups plain yogurt, regular or low-fat
2 tablespoons honey or brown sugar
Pinch of freshly ground white pepper
1 to 2 teaspoons ground cinnamon, or to taste

1. In a small bowl, combine the yogurt, honey or brown sugar, and white pepper and mix well. Sprinkle the cinnamon over the top of the mixture and swirl in.

2. Transfer to a bowl, cover with plastic wrap, refrigerate, and serve chilled.

Variation

For minted honey yogurt, substitute 1 tablespoon chopped fresh mint for the cinnamon.

Apricot and Dijon Dip

Makes about 1 cup

1 cup apricot preserves
1 teaspoon white wine vinegar
2 tablespoons Dijon-style mustard
Pinch of freshly ground white pepper

1. In a small saucepan, warm the preserves over medium-low heat and pour into a blender.

2. Add the vinegar, mustard, and pepper and blend until smooth.

3. Transfer into a serving bowl and serve warm.

Serve this delicious dip with French Fried Beet, Zucchini, and Onion Rounds (page 158), or with Roasted Curried Potato Wedges (page 160).

Homemade
ACCOMPANIMENTS

Homemade Accompaniments

It's always a treat to serve homemade accompaniments with your homemade spreads, toppers, and dips. Here are some simple recipes for things to spread on, mound on top of, and dunk. What's more, they have been selected to pair with the recipes throughout this book.

Bruschetta
(Italian-Style Garlic Toast)

Makes 8 to 10 slices, depending on size of loaf

1 large loaf of country-style bread (see Note), cut into thick slices
2 large cloves garlic, halved
Extra virgin olive oil
Coarse salt
Dried oregano or other strong herb, such as rosemary, thyme, or sage, finely crushed
Crushed red pepper flakes (optional)

1. Prepare a charcoal grill or the broiler.

2. Grill or broil the slices of bread until the edges begin to turn golden brown. Turn and repeat on the other side.

3. Rub the bread slices on one side with garlic halves. Discard the used garlic.

4. Drizzle or brush on a scant amount of olive oil. Sprinkle with a little salt, dried herb, and crushed red pepper flakes if using.

Note: Choose any type of country bread, such as an interestingly shaped loaf encrusted with seeds, or one that is made with olives or herbs, such as a rosemary bread. Or try an egg, sourdough, wheat bread, or Italian ciabatta, made with olive oil.

Rustic Croûtes
(Crisp Herb Toast)

$^1/_3$ cup extra virgin olive oil

$^1/_4$ cup finely chopped mixed fresh herbs, such as basil, chervil, parsley,
and chives

2 baguette-style loaves, about 3 inches in diameter, sliced on the diagonal
or in rounds about $^1/_3$ inch thick

2 large cloves garlic, halved (optional; see Note)

Coarse salt (optional)

A few turns of the peppermill (optional)

1. Preheat the oven to 325°F.

2. In a small bowl, combine the olive oil and herbs and set aside. If using garlic, lightly rub the bread slices on one side. Discard the used garlic. Brush the bread slices lightly with the oil-herb mixture on both sides.

3. Lay the bread slices in a single layer on the baking sheet and sprinkle with coarse salt and a few turns of the peppermill if using.

4. Bake until very crisp and brown if desired, 7 to 10 minutes. Serve immediately or store in an airtight container.

Note: The garlic in this recipe should be reduced or eliminated if the accompanying spread, topper, or dip already has plenty of garlic.

Variations

Rustic Pesto Croûtes

Eliminate the fresh herbs and combine 2 to 3 tablespoons pesto (see pages 113–116 for recipes) with equal amounts of extra virgin olive oil. Spread a little of the pesto mixture on the bread slices, then bake.

Asian Flavor Croûtes

Instead of olive oil, use mostly light sesame oil with just a teaspoon of dark sesame oil mixed in. For the herb combination, use minced scallion (white and green parts) and minced cilantro.

Crispy Buttered Toasts

Instead of olive oil, combine equal amounts of butter and oil, or use all clarified butter. Eliminate the garlic.

Crostini
(Small Italian-Style Toasts)

Makes 24 to 36 slices, depending on size of loaf

**1 baguette (see Note), about 3 inches in diameter, sliced on the diagonal
or in rounds about $1/_3$ inch thick**
2 large cloves garlic, halved
Extra virgin olive oil (optional)

1. Preheat the oven to 375°F.

2. Lightly rub the baguette slices on one side with the garlic halves. Discard the used garlic. Brush the slices very lightly on both sides with the olive oil, if using.

3. Place in a single layer on a baking sheet. Bake until golden on the edges but slightly soft on the inside, 3 to 5 minutes.

Note: Choose a freshly baked, very crusty loaf, such as a French mini baguette or a narrow baguette-type Italian loaf.

Crispy Falafel Rounds

Makes about 20 rounds

One 14-ounce can chickpeas (garbanzo beans), drained
1 large clove garlic, pressed
$1/_2$ teaspoon ground coriander
$1/_2$ teaspoon ground cumin
1 large egg yolk
1 cup fresh white bread crumbs
Vegetable oil for frying

1. In the bowl of a food processor fitted with the metal blade, combine the chickpeas, garlic, coriander, cumin, and egg yolk. Process to a smooth paste. Add the bread crumbs and pulse a few times to combine.

2. Roll the mixture into approximately 20 balls and press into rounded patties.

3. In a large, heavy skillet, heat 1 to 2 tablespoons of the oil over medium-high heat until very hot. Cook the rounds in batches of 6 to 8, pressing lightly to flatten slightly, until golden brown, about 8 minutes. Drain on paper towels for a few seconds. Heat more oil to very hot before adding more rounds to the pan.

4. Serve immediately or place in the oven to keep warm. Serve within 15 minutes of cooking.

Grilled or Broiled Vegetable Slices

Vegetables such as sliced eggplant and zucchini, halved tomatoes, thickly sliced onions, carrots halved lengthwise, or asparagus spears, all skewered together on wooden skewers that have been presoaked in water

Olive oil, vinaigrette, or marinade of choice, enough to brush all the vegetables on both sides

Salt

Freshly ground black pepper

$1/4$ to 1 cup chopped fresh herbs

1. Prepare a charcoal grill or heat the broiler.

2. Season the oil, vinaigrette, or marinade with salt and pepper to taste. Baste the vegetables with the oil, vinaigrette, or marinade and let marinate for 30 minutes. Season to taste with salt and pepper. Grill or broil for 2 to 3 minutes per side. The vegetables should remain somewhat firm and crisp, not quite cooked throughout.

3. Transfer to a serving platter in a single layer, sprinkle with herbs, and let cool to room temperature.

Fried Green Tomatoes

Makes 15 to 20 slices

3 tablespoons all-purpose flour
1/2 cup yellow cornmeal
1 teaspoon salt
1 teaspoon freshly ground black pepper
2 large egg yolks mixed with 1 teaspoon water
1/2 cup canola or vegetable oil
4 medium-size green tomatoes (see Note), sliced 1/2 inch thick

1. In a small bowl, combine the flour, cornmeal, salt, and pepper. Pour onto a plate and spread to cover the plate completely. Place the egg yolks in a shallow dish.

2. In a large, heavy skillet or sauté pan, heat the oil over medium-high heat until very hot.

3. Meanwhile, dip each slice of tomato into the egg yolk, allowing the excess to drip back into the dish. Then press both sides of the tomato slices into the cornmeal mixture to coat well. Fry in batches in the hot oil until golden brown on both sides, about 5 minutes.

4. Place the tomato slices on paper towels to absorb any excess oil. Serve immediately while still hot, or place in a warm oven until all the tomato slices have all been fried. Serve hot from the oven.

Note: If green tomatoes are not available, use firm red tomatoes.

French Fried Beet, Zucchini, and Onion Rounds

This recipe can also be used to French fry or tempura fry any of the following: sweet potatoes or yams, green beans, cauliflower or broccoli florets, or yellow crookneck squash.

2 pounds whole beets, boiled to firm-tender (12 to 15 minutes), cooled and sliced ¹/₃ inch thick
³/₄ pound zucchini, sliced on the diagonal ¹/₃ inch thick
2 large sweet onions (Maui or Vidalia, if desired), peeled and ends trimmed, sliced ¹/₃ inch thick
1¹/₂ cups all-purpose flour
2 large eggs, slightly beaten
¹/₂ cup dry white wine or chicken broth
¹/₄ teaspoon hot or sweet paprika
1 cup canola oil, or more as needed
1 cup pure olive oil or vegetable oil, or more as needed
Coarse salt
1 tablespoon chopped fresh herbs, such as basil, mint, flat-leaf parsley, or cilantro, or to taste
Lemon halves for garnish

1. Place the vegetables on paper towels to drain.

2. Whisk the flour, eggs, and the wine or broth together. Strain to remove any flour lumps. Sprinkle in the paprika and continue whisking to mix well.

3. In a large, heavy skillet, heat about ¹/₃ cup of both oils over high heat until very hot. Meanwhile, dip the beet, zucchini, and onion slices in the batter, coating both sides well. Slide the slices into the hot oil, filling the bottom of the pan, and fry until the batter is browned, 3 to 5 minutes. Remove using a slotted utensil and drain on paper towels. Repeat until all the slices are fried. (Add more oil as necessary, so that the vegetable slices are immersed while cooking. Heat to very hot before adding more slices. If the vegetables are only partially immersed in hot oil, turning may be necessary.)

4. Sprinkle immediately with salt to taste and the chopped herbs. Serve immediately with lemon halves on the side.

Plantain Chips

Makes 20 to 24 chips

2 unripe (green) plantains (see Note), peeled and thinly sliced
Peanut or vegetable oil for deep-frying
Coarse salt
Freshly ground black pepper

1. Rinse the plantain slices under cold water and pat dry with paper towels.

2. In a deep-fryer or heavy skillet, heat the oil to 375°F, or hot enough to fry a bread cube to golden brown in about 1 minute.

3. Slide the plantain pieces into the hot oil. Fry until golden and tender, about 5 minutes. Place on paper towels to absorb any excess oil. Continue until all the plantain pieces are fried. Keep hot in the oven.

4. Sprinkle with coarse salt and pepper to taste. Serve hot.

Note: Plantains are usually available in Latin markets.

Variation

Use sweet potatoes or yams instead of plantains.

Roasted Curried Potato Wedges

Makes 32 to 40 wedges

2 tablespoons canola or safflower oil
4 large russet, yellow fin, purple, or sweet potatoes (about 1¹/₂ pounds),
   washed and peeled (optional)
2 teaspoons mild or hot curry powder (Madras or best quality available),
   or to taste
Coarse salt

1. Preheat the oven to 400°F. Pour the oil into a roasting pan and heat in the oven for 5 minutes.

2. Cut each potato into 8 to 10 wedges. Add to the roasting pan and toss in the oil to coat well. Sprinkle with the curry powder. Roast the potatoes until the wedges are golden brown and done throughout, about 30 minutes; turn once after 15 minutes.

3. Transfer to a serving dish and sprinkle with coarse salt to taste. Serve hot.

Crispy Mushrooms

Makes 25 to 30 slices

2 large eggs, beaten
Pinch of salt
Pinch of freshly ground black pepper
1 cup unseasoned dried bread crumbs
Vegetable oil for deep-frying
2 pounds extra-large fresh mushrooms, trimmed, cleaned, and sliced
$1/2$ inch thick (or use smaller mushrooms, whole)
2 tablespoons fresh lemon juice
2 tablespoons finely chopped flat-leaf parsley

1. In a small mixing bowl, combine the eggs and salt and pepper. Pour into a shallow bowl.

2. Spread the bread crumbs evenly on a plate.

3. In a deep-fryer or large, heavy skillet, heat oil to 350°F, or hot enough to fry a bread cube to golden brown in 1 minute.

4. Meanwhile, dip the mushroom slices into the egg and coat on all sides. Then press into the bread crumbs and coat well.

5. Fry the mushroom slices until golden brown and crisp, 2 to 3 minutes. Place on paper towels to absorb any excess oil. Transfer the mushrooms to a serving platter, sprinkle with the lemon juice and chopped parsley, and season with salt and pepper to taste. Serve immediately.

Chips and Crackers

Herb or Spice Pita Chips

Makes about 100 chips

1 package fresh pita bread (8 loaves), layers split apart, each layer cut into
   6 wedges (8 wedges for smaller chips)
Olive oil, canola oil, or melted butter for brushing

For Herb Chips

2 tablespoons dried herbs, such as thyme, tarragon, dill, basil, chervil,
   or chives

For Spice Chips

3 tablespoons hot or mild spice blend of choice, or 2 tablespoons chili powder
   (ancho if available) or mild or hot curry powder

1. Preheat the oven to 300°F.

2. Lightly brush the pita wedges with oil or butter. Dust with dried herbs or spices.

3. Bake until the chips are crisp, 5 to 7 minutes. Serve warm or at room temperature. Or store in an airtight container.

Bagel Chips

Makes about 60 chips

Day-old bagels, one dozen, any flavor, thinly sliced
Melted butter for brushing
Savory seasoning mix like garlic, onion, salt, or herb

1. Preheat the oven to 300°F.

2. Lightly brush the bagel slices with melted butter. Dust with seasoning.

3. Bake until the chips are crisp, 5 to 7 minutes. Serve warm or at room temperature. Or store in an airtight container.

Low-Fat Baked Tortilla Chips

Makes 60 to 80 chips

10 fresh flour tortillas (fat-reduced if available), each cut into 6 to 8 wedges
1 tablespoon ground cumin or chili powder (ancho if available), optional

1. Preheat the oven to 300°F.

2. Place the tortilla wedges on a baking sheet. Sprinkle with cumin or chili powder if using. Place in the oven until dry and crisp, 5 to 7 minutes.

3. Serve immediately. Or store in an airtight container until ready to use. Rewarm before serving.

Tortilla Corn Chips

Makes about 120 chips

Corn or peanut oil for deep-frying
Twenty 6-inch blue, white, or yellow corn tortillas, each cut into 6 wedges
Coarse salt

1. In a deep-fryer or large, heavy saucepan, heat the oil to 375°F, or hot enough to fry a piece of the tortilla in 1 minute.

2. Carefully add the tortillas to the hot oil and deep-fry until crisp, about 2 minutes. Don't crowd the pan. Place on paper towels to absorb any excess oil, and season with salt to taste.

3. Serve immediately or store in an airtight container. Reheat in a hot oven for a minute or two before serving.

Variation

For tortilla strips, cut corn tortillas into 1-inch strips instead of wedges.

Plain or Spicy Potato Chips

Makes about 200 chips

Vegetable or peanut oil for deep-frying
8 large russet potatoes, peeled and sliced thin on a mandoline, the blade side
of a steel grater, or with a very sharp heavy-bladed knife
Salt
For Spicy Potato Chips: $^1/_4$ cup chili powder (ancho if available)

1. In a deep-fryer or large, heavy skillet, heat the oil to 375°F, or until a slice of potato sizzles when immersed and is golden and done in about 1 minute.

2. Fry the chips in batches until crisp and golden, 1 to 2 minutes. Remove with a slotted utensil. Place on paper towels to absorb any excess oil. While still hot, sprinkle with salt to taste, and if making Spicy Potato Chips, dust with chili powder.

3. Serve immediately or store in an airtight container.

Goat Cheese Crackers

Makes about 40 small crackers

1 cup all-purpose flour
$^1/_4$ cup ($^1/_2$ stick) unsalted butter, room temperature
5 to 7 ounces unaged chèvre (see page 23), such as Montrachet, crumbled
3 tablespoons sour cream, regular or low-fat
1 large egg white, beaten
Coarse salt

1. In the bowl of a food processor fitted with the metal or plastic blade, combine the flour, butter, cheese, and sour cream and process to a smooth dough.

2. Roll the mixture into 2 logs about 1 inch thick. Wrap in plastic wrap or wax paper and chill thoroughly for 1 hour or more.

3. Preheat the oven to 350°F.

4. With a very sharp knife, cut the logs into $^1/_4$ inch thick slices. Place the slices on a baking sheet. Prick each once with the tines of a fork. Brush with the egg white and sprinkle with a scant amount of coarse salt.

5. Bake until lightly browned, 12 to 15 minutes. Let cool on a rack to room temperature before serving.

Homemade Vegetable Chips

Makes about 200 chips

3 parsnips, peeled
4 to 6 very large carrots, peeled
3 cooked beets, peeled
1 sweet potato, peeled
Vegetable oil for deep-frying
Coarse salt
A few turns of the peppermill

1. Using a mandoline, the blade side of a grater, or a sharp knife, slice the vegetables very thin. Lay the vegetable slices on paper towels, cover with several layers, and press down to extract any moisture.

2. In a deep-fryer or large, heavy skillet, heat the oil to 375°F, or until a vegetable slice placed in the oil is done in 1 minute. Fry the vegetable slices in batches until golden brown and crisp, 1 to 2 minutes. Using a slotted utensil, remove the slices and place on paper towels to absorb any excess oil. Dust with salt and a few turns of the peppermill to taste.

3. Serve a mix of all the vegetable varieties while hot or at room temperature.

Polenta Crisps
(Cornmeal Crackers)

Makes 40 medium crackers

Vegetable oil cooking spray, or 2 teaspoons melted butter
3 cups water
Salt
1 1/2 cups yellow cornmeal
1/2 to 1 teaspoon chili powder, to taste (optional)
1/4 cup (1/2 stick) unsalted butter, melted

1. Preheat the oven to 400°F.

2. Lightly coat 2 baking sheets with cooking spray or brush lightly with 2 teaspoons melted butter. Set aside.

3. In a medium saucepan, bring 3 cups of lightly salted water to a boil. Add the cornmeal in a thin but steady stream, stirring constantly while pouring. Stir in the chili powder if using, and cook for 5 minutes, stirring constantly. Remove the saucepan from the heat. Stir in the 1/4 cup melted butter.

4. Scoop heaping tablespoons of the cornmeal batter mixture onto the baking sheets. Press to flatten slightly. Bake until the edges begin to brown and turn crisp, about 30 minutes. Transfer to a rack to cool.

Scallion Pancakes

Makes about 40 pancakes

$^1/_2$ **cup all-purpose flour**
$^1/_2$ **cup whole-wheat flour (very fresh)**
$^1/_2$ **teaspoon salt**
$^1/_2$ **teaspoon freshly ground black pepper**
4 large eggs, slightly beaten
1$^1/_2$ cups milk
2 tablespoons unsalted butter, melted and cooled to room temperature
$^1/_2$ **cup finely chopped scallions, light green and dark green parts**
Canola oil for frying

1. In a medium bowl, stir together both flours, the salt, and pepper and set aside.

2. In another medium bowl, whisk together the eggs, milk, and butter. Gradually add the dry ingredients, whisking until all the ingredients are incorporated and smooth. Stir in the scallions. Set the batter aside for 1 hour at room temperature.

3. In a crêpe pan or a small omelet or sauté pan, heat about $^1/_4$ teaspoon oil over medium heat. Remove the pan from the heat and tip or use a brush to coat the bottom completely with oil. Wipe out any excess oil with a paper towel. Spoon 2 tablespoons of the batter into the hot pan and tilt the pan to quickly spread the batter evenly. Return the pan to the heat and cook until the pancake is browned on the bottom, about 1 minute. Gently but quickly turn the pancake with your fingers and allow the other side to brown, about 1 minute more. Slide the pancake onto a baking sheet.

4. Repeat with the remaining batter until all the pancakes are done, stacking the pancakes on top of one another and covering with aluminum foil. Serve warm or at room temperature.

Fresh Cucumber and Zucchini Cups

Makes about 20 to 30 cups

1 to 2 hothouse cucumbers, peeled if desired and sliced $3/4$ to 1 inch thick
1 to 2 medium to large zucchini, peeled if desired and sliced $3/4$ to 1 inch thick

1. Scoop out the centers of the slices with a $1/2$ teaspoon or small melon baller, leaving a space to fill. Do not cut through the bottom of the slices.

2. Place on a tray and fill with toppers of choice. Serve immediately or cover with plastic wrap and chill until ready to serve.

Potato Skins

4 small to medium baking potatoes, or 8 tiny red-skinned potatoes,
well scrubbed, dried, and halved
Extra virgin olive oil or melted butter for brushing
Salt
Freshly ground black pepper

1. Preheat the oven to 350°F.

2. Scoop out the centers of the potato halves, leaving about $1/3$ of the potato intact. (Do not break the skin.) Place on a baking sheet. Brush the inside with the oil or butter. Sprinkle lightly with salt and pepper.

3. Bake until the potatoes are tender throughout, about 35 minutes. Test tiny red potatoes for doneness after 25 minutes. Serve hot with toppers of choice.

Crispy Won Ton Strips

Makes about 150 strips

Canola or peanut oil for deep-frying
1 package of won ton skins (about 50 per pack), see Note

1. In a large, heavy skillet or a deep-fryer, heat the oil over high heat until very hot but not smoking.

2. Cut the won ton skins into strips and deep-fry until golden, about 1 minute. Place on paper towels to absorb any excess oil.

3. Serve immediately. Or store in an airtight container. Reheat in the oven if desired before serving.

Note: You can find won ton skins in the cold section of the market where fresh pastas are kept, or in Asian food markets.

Index